American Book Company's

SAT READING

TEST PREPARATION GUIDE

Revised September 2007

Dr. Frank J. Pintozzi, Project Director
Zuzana Urbanek, Project Coordinator

Maria L. Struder
Teresa Valentine

Contributing Writers:
Kim Hill, Dave Jordan, Michael Kabel
Margaret DuPree

AMERICAN BOOK COMPANY
P O BOX 2638
WOODSTOCK GEORGIA 30188-1383
Toll Free: 1 (888) 264-5877   Phone: 770-928-2834
Toll Free Fax: 1 (866) 827-3240
Web site: www.americanbookcompany.com

ACKNOWLEDGEMENTS

The authors would like to gratefully acknowledge the technical contributions of Marsha Torrens.

The authors would also like to thank Mary Stoddard for her work with the graphics in this book.

A special thanks to Zuzana Urbanek, and Margaret DuPree for their meticulous attention to detail in editing this book for publication.

This product/publication includes images from CorelDRAW 9 and 11 which are protected by the copyright laws of the United States, Canada, and elsewhere. Used under license.

1st Edition December 2005
2nd Edition September 2007

Printed in the United States of America
09/07

SAT Reading Test Preparation Guide
Table of Contents

SAT Reading Test Preparation Guide
Preface

The SAT Reading Test Preparation Guide will help students preparing to take the SAT Test. The College Board Association's expanded requirements for the SAT Reading Test are covered in this book. The materials presented here will also help students who want to retake the SAT Reading Test to improve their previous score.

This book contains several sections: 1) general information about the book, 2) a complete reading diagnostic test, 3) an evaluation chart, 4) chapters that teach the concepts and skills that improve readiness for the SAT Reading Test, and 5) three practice tests. Answers to the tests and exercises are in a separate manual.

We welcome your comments and suggestions. Please contact the authors at

American Book Company
PO Box 2638
Woodstock, GA 30188-1383

Toll Free: 1 (888) 264-5877
Phone: (770) 928-2834
Fax: (770) 928-7483
web site: www.americanbookcompany.com

ABOUT THE AUTHORS

Dr. Frank J. Pintozzi is a former Professor of Education at Kennesaw (GA) State University. For over 28 years, he has taught English and reading at the high school and college levels as well as in teacher preparation courses in language arts and social studies. In addition to writing and editing state standard-specific texts for high school exit and end of course exams, he has edited and written numerous college textbooks.

Maria L. Struder received a BA in English from Kennesaw State University (GA). She has taught writing skills at the college level and is currently enrolled in the Masters in Professional Writing Program at KSU.

Teresa Valentine is currently enrolled in the Masters of Arts in Professional Writing Program at Kennesaw State University, Kennesaw, GA. She has worked as a writing consultant coaching undergraduates from all disciplines in composition writing.

TEST-TAKING TIPS

1 **Complete the chapters and practice tests in this book.** This text will help you review the skills for SAT Reading preparation.

2 **Be prepared.** Get a good night's sleep the day before your exam. Eat a well-balanced meal containing plenty of proteins and carbohydrates.

3 **Arrive early.** Allow yourself at least 15–20 minutes to find your room and get settled. Then you can relax before the exam, and you won't feel rushed.

4 **Keep your thoughts positive.** Tell yourself you will do well on the exam.

5 **Practice relaxation techniques.** Some students become overly worried about exams. Before or during the test they may perspire heavily, develop an upset stomach, or have shortness of breath. If you feel any of these symptoms, talk to a close friend or see a counselor. They will suggest ways to deal with test anxiety.

Here are some quick ways to relieve test anxiety:

- Imagine yourself in your favorite place. Let yourself sit there and relax.
- Do a body scan. Tense and relax each part of your body starting with your toes and ending with your forehead.
- **The 3-12-6 method:** Inhale slowly for 3 seconds. Hold your breath for 12 seconds, and then exhale slowly for 6 seconds.

6 **Read directions carefully.** If you don't understand them, ask the proctor for further explanation before the exam starts.

7 **Answer easy questions first.** Both easy and hard questions count equally, so if you are sure about the correct answer, do the easy questions first.

8 **Use your best approach for answering the questions.** Some test-takers like to skim the questions and answers before reading the example. Others prefer to read the example before looking at the possible answers. Decide which approach works best for you.

9 **Choose the best answer.** Choose answers you're sure are correct. If you are not sure of an answer, take an educated guess. Eliminate choices that are definitely wrong, and choose from the remaining answers.

10 **Use your answer sheet correctly.** Make sure the number of your question matches the number on your answer sheet. In this way, you will record your answers correctly. If you need to change your answer, completely erase it. Smudges or stray marks may affect the grading of your exams, particularly if they are scored by a computer. If your answers are on a computerized grading sheet, make sure the answers are dark. The scanner may skip over answers that are marked too lightly.

11 **Check your answers.** If you have the opportunity before time is called, review each section to make sure you have chosen the best responses. Change answers only if you are sure they are wrong.

SAT Reading Test Preparation Guide
Diagnostic Test

Section I

24 Questions

Time – 25 minutes

Directions: For each question in this section, select the best answer from among the given choices.

Each sentence below has one or two blanks, each blank indicating that something has been omitted. Beneath the sentence are five choices, labeled A through E. Choose the word or combination of words that, when placed in the sentence, *best* fits the sentence's meaning.

> **Example:** Bob worried it was only a matter of time before Katie_____; she'd been enthusiastic about the plan yesterday, but he expected her to feel differently once she gave the idea serious _____.
>
> A. wavered… decision
> B. obliged… hesitation
> C. demurred… consideration
> D. argued… rethinking
> E. exited… reconciliation
>
> The correct answer is *C*.

1. Green algae remains_____ until rain revives it, growing again in sunlight-rich environments.
   A. dormant   D. intelligent
   B. excited   E. small
   C. active

2. Exercises that increase heart and breathing rates for an extended amount of time are said to be _____, increasing good oxygen flow through the body.
   A. short   D. aerobic
   B. easy   E. of long duration
   C. arduous

3. In previous centuries, women frequently found marriage their only path to financial _____; modern attitudes regarding their _____ with men had not yet taken root through much of the world.
   A. security… equality
   B. growth… inferiority
   C. wisdom… status
   D. misfortune… depending
   E. collapse... work

4. Because penguins' body systems are so _____, even a small _____ in habitat temperature could have disastrous effects.
   A. round… dip
   B. reptile… loose
   C. fragile… fluctuation
   D. loose… alteration
   E. cute… growth

5. Wanting to end the dispute, union representatives proposed a(n) _____ with team owners that they hoped would be _____ to everyone involved.
   A. rest… optimistic
   B. compromise… satisfactory
   C. alliance… hostile
   D. goal… unwieldy
   E. extension… acceptable

6. President Wilson knew that world politics had changed and that the United States could no longer remain_____ on its side of the Atlantic; entering World War I was a dramatic step in drawing the nation towards a more _____ role in international affairs.
   A. complacent… sluggish
   B. active…. responsible
   C. comfortable… concerned
   D. alone… confined
   E. isolated… assertive

7. Jack London's novels, though considered _____ by modern literary standards, nonetheless contain elements of symbolism and allegory on a par with much of contemporary fiction.
   A. simplistic   D. concave
   B. complex   E. sentimental
   C. complicated

8. Jay wanted his friends to consider him _____ despite his lack of formal education, going so far as to read vocabulary-building lists and digest reading materials.
   A. naive   D. erudite
   B. fastidious   E. crude
   C. responsible

The passages following are followed by questions based on content. Questions following a pair of related passages may also concern how the passages relate to one another. Answer the questions below on the basis of what is *stated* or *implied* in the passages as well as any introductory material provided.

Questions 9 & 10 are based on this passage:

Scientists noted a difference between the wild camels of the Gobi desert and the domesticated camels of the same region. The wild camels had a healthier growth of **(5)**hair on their knee caps and wider space between their humps than their tamed cousins. In comparing the two varieties' genetic material, they found great difference in their genetic codes, leading **(10)**the scientists to believe in the wild camel as a new species. The theory may explain why the wild camel can thrive on the salty water found in its desert environment, devoid of competition from **(15)**other animals that must look elsewhere in the desert for life-sustaining hydration.

9. The passage suggests that wild camels are heartier than domesticated camels because
   A. they haven't been exposed to the debilitating effects of fresh water.
   B. nature has decided to give them more hair and a wider space between humps.
   C. their genetic code allows them to survive on salty desert water.
   D. they evolved first.
   E. other animals force them to fight for the water they drink.

10. The author mentions the wild camels' knee hair and wide space between humps in order to
    A. give several examples of differences in wild and domesticated camels.
    B. provide vivid detail.
    C. show how evolution can result in new characteristics.
    D. demonstrate the effects of drinking salt water.
    E. show what scientists consider evidence.

Questions 11 & 12 are based on this passage:

There are several common types of bias to consider, not only in judging the statements of others but in our own views. People are usually too quick to disregard **(5)**evidence that does not fit with their point of view; on the other hand, people are also often too quick to accept, without qualification, evidence with which they agree. In addition, people often propose **(10)**that evidence supports their position when in fact it may not actually do so. When weighing evidence, one should always consider its source, whether it is in dispute or verifiably true, and whether it **(15)**serves to support the author's view-point.

11. The passage is primarily concerned with

- A. the unreliable nature of evidence in the hands of the opinionated.
- B. explaining how bias may taint the presentation and acceptance of evidence.
- C. listing the several types of bias.
- D. instructing how to avoid bias in everyday life.
- E. offering evidence suggesting how bias can disrupt arguments.

12. The passage suggests that people sometimes agree with bias because

- A. it sometimes lists verifiable facts.
- B. people need opinions.
- C. sometimes bias can be a good thing.
- D. it supports opinions they already have.
- E. evidence is often unreliable.

Questions 13 through 24 are based on the following passage:
The following passage, by J.H. McBride, was published in an issue of The Scientific Monthly *in 1915.*

Our educational authorities, though in many instances interested in physical development of the young, have not given the subject the important place in their program that it deserves. **(5)**This is not wholly due to indifference, but largely to their ideals that were derived from classical-ascetic standards.

In the medieval ideal the human body was animal and sinful, to be despised and repressed. **(10)**The mind was said to be the spiritual element in man, representing the immortal part of his nature, and therefore was the only part worthy of attention in an educational system. From the fall of the Roman Empire to the later **(15)**nineteenth century this ideal dominated education.

The medieval universities, including Oxford and Cambridge, provided only for mental training. Their education was intended for those who were **(20)**to follow the professions or to become scholars or gentlemen of leisure. Education was not intended to prepare the great mass of men for the every-day work of life.

While only indirectly related to my subject, it is **(25)**interesting to recall that there was in this country in the early nineteenth century much opposition to the establishment of common schools for the masses. It was claimed that those who belonged to the working classes did not **(30)**need to be educated. Our own colleges and universities were originally founded on the old classical-ascetic model, so that the spirit of the medieval period survived in the educational plan of this country. It is only in recent decades that **(35)**these institutions have begun to depart from the older, formal, classical methods that made education a privilege of the few, the average man being deprived of the advantages of the training that he needed. Because of this the humble **(40)**millions of men and women who wove and spun, and fed and housed the world were left out of the educational scheme.

Some years ago a London weekly paper, which speaks for the conservative class of England, in **(45)**discussing certain suggested innovations in English higher education, said that the great merit of education at Oxford and Cambridge was that it was "absolutely useless." By this it was probably meant that the education was for a **(50)**chosen few, was not intended to prepare men for the practical work of life and was essentially and only an intellectual and cultural training.

The change of attitude that is seen in our day is due chiefly to two great discoveries: the **(55)**re-discovery of the human body and its relation to our mentality and the discovery of the mind of the child and youth. We have found that man is an animal who graduated from caves and dugouts and to whom even barbarism was a lade **(60)**and great achievement. That the human body was made by the experiences of that rude life, and that since then we have made no change in it except to stand on two feet. Neither have we added one nerve cell or fiber to our brains since **(65)**the day when the cave was home and uncooked food the daily diet.

The conception of man as an animal has led to a study of him as such. Educators as a class now concede that the physical man must be **(70)**considered as an essential part of their scheme, that the brain is an organ of the body among other organs, and is subject to the same laws and influenced by similar conditions.

The influence of the mind upon the body is a **(75)**commonplace of psychology, but the influence of the body upon the mind is of equal importance, though less frequently emphasized.

Whatever one's theory of the nature of mind, it must be considered in relation to the brain as the **(80)**organ of its expression. The mind has, too, a broader base than the brain, for every organ of the body has some share in the mental functions. Every physician knows that physical disease lowers the quality of the thinking and, with the **(85)**exception of a few geniuses like Darwin and Leopardi, it makes impossible intellectual work of a high order. Disorders of the internal organs rob the brain of nourishment and weaken it, and by obtruding their morbidness upon it they batter **(90)**down its resistances and lower the thinking power.

13. "Our educational authorities" (line 1) refers to
   A. students.
   B. parents.
   C. teachers and administrators.
   D. scientists and researchers.
   E. the author.

14. What conclusion can be drawn from the information in the second paragraph?
   A. People in medieval times did not perform physical labor.
   B. The idea of physical education did not exist until modern times.
   C. People in medieval times were corrupt.
   D. The ideals of the Roman Empire greatly influence modern education
   E. Education in medieval times was only for the wealthy.

15. According to the author, the human body was regarded as _____ in medieval times (lines 8–9).
   A. mysterious   D. ungodly
   B. weak   E. powerful
   C. perfect

16. The author mentions that some Americans opposed the establishment of public schools for the masses (paragraph 4) in order to
   A. show how medieval ideas are similar to modern ideas.
   B. explain why public schools were prevented from opening.
   C. show that the English educational system is superior.
   D. argue in favor of private schools.
   E. show how attitudes towards education have changed over time.

17. The word "concede" (line 69) is closest in meaning to which of the following words?
   A. admit   D. predict
   B. surrender   E. wonder
   C. disagree

18. The word "scheme" (line 42), as it is used in the passage, is closest in meaning to which of the following words?

    A. conspiracy   D. class
    B. system   E. privilege
    C. trap

19. Based on the information in the fourth paragraph, it can be inferred that

    A. the English educational system has remained the same since it was created.
    B. English universities are centered on providing practical training for students.
    C. the author believes that education should not be exclusively for the upper class.
    D. the author believes that nearly everyone went to college in the 19th century.
    E. those who belong to the working class do not need to be educated.

20. The word "obtruding" (line 89) most nearly means

    A. excluding.   D. welcoming.
    B. forcing.   E. avoiding.
    C. lowering.

21. The author's main argument is that

    A. people in medieval times thought the human body was sinful.
    B. physical education is as important as mental education.
    C. education should be focused purely on the mind.
    D. American education should be focused on the classics.
    E. a quality public education should be available to all.

22. Which of the following statements is NOT an idea expressed by the author?

    A. Physical health can affect the mental health of a person.
    B. Like other organs, the human brain can be influenced by certain conditions.
    C. The human mind and the human body are separate and isolated from each other.
    D. The concept of the mind extends beyond the physical limitations of the brain.
    E. The human body is basically the same as it was in cave-dwelling days.

23. Which of the following best explains the purpose of this passage?

    A. to justify an old way of thinking
    B. to apply new discoveries to traditional ideals
    C. to evaluate another person's analysis of education
    D. to explain a process
    E. to describe a personal experience

24. The tone of this passage is mostly

    A. scholarly.
    B. impassioned.
    C. neutral.
    D. flippant.
    E. scornful.

Section II

23 Questions

Time – 25 minutes

> Each sentence below has one or two blanks, each blank indicating that something has been omitted. Beneath the sentence are five choices, labeled A through E. Choose the word or combination of words that, when placed in the sentence, *best* fits the sentence's meaning.
>
> **Example:** By definition, meticulous workers are almost _____ with detail, going to great pains to get the finer points of a task in good order.
>
> | | | | |
> |---|---|---|---|
> | A. | obsessed | D. | interested |
> | B. | remiss | E. | infatuated |
> | C. | casual | | |
>
> The correct answer is A.

1. The legislation was met by almost unanimous _____ in the Senate; the hopes of the bill's authors were quickly dashed.

   A. approval   D. confusion

   B. dissent   E. embarrassment

   C. applause

2. A timeline is a series of events displayed in _____ order, irrespective of importance or personal perspective.

   A. reverse   D. scientific

   B. real-time   E. random

   C. chronological

3. The musician always _____ requests by members of the audience; he believed in _____ to the public's tastes at every opportunity.

   A. denied… accepting

   B. accepted… ignoring

   C. wondered at… a challenge

   D. stifled… heeding

   E. accommodated… appealing

4. Many modern autobiographies lose _____ due to the celebrity of their subjects; all too often, the subject's desire for _____ publicity leads to omission of facts.

   A. veracity… positive

   B. honesty… negative

   C. favor… concise

   D. popularity… true

   E. tenacity… growing

5. We will not _____ to the demands of the student protestors. There are issues of public _____ and welfare that preclude their wishes.

   A. stoop… approval

   B. acquiesce… stability

   C. adjourn… taste

   D. disagree… hopes

   E. waver… affection

The passages below are followed by questions based on content. Questions following a pair of related passages may also concern how the passages relate to one another. Answer the questions below on the basis of what is stated or implied in the passages as well as any introductory material provided.

Questions 6–9 are based on the following passages:

Passage 1

Sensationalism in the news sprang up at the end of the 19th century and increased readership for newspapers. Famous publishing tycoons Joseph (5)Pulitzer and William Randolph Hearst battled with one another to increase circulation and advertising revenue, developing a reporting style that focused less on facts and more on human-interest stories, (10)especially those that were scandalous or astounding. Today, one might argue that responsible journalism—which focuses on facts that can be verified and presents news in a relatively unbiased manner— (15)has superseded the exaggeration of stories that were the hallmark of so-called "yellow journalism." However, the lurid and sensational stories are always at the top of the list. Some say that this proves (20)yellow journalism is alive and well in all media, but today, these kinds of stories are usually reported in a factual and balanced style.

Passage 2

The popular tabloid market is where yellow journalism truly thrives today. On the newsstands and in the supermarkets, papers like the *The National Enquirer*, *The* (25)*Star*, *The Globe*, and *The Examiner* proclaim in bold headlines that "Elvis is Alive," "Woman Gives Birth to Alien Twins," and "Bigfoot Is Captured!" While no one would argue that the tabloids' (30)reporting standards are less than rigorous by today's practices, these publications seem to fill an incessant need the public has for "junk food news." Although many people won't admit to (35)reading—much less buying—these tabloids, the fact remains that even though tabloid circulation has been falling in recent years, it remains at tens of millions of copies per year. *Someone* is certainly (40)reading these newspapers!

6. Both passages are concerned with the
   A. continued popularity of "yellow" journalism.
   B. role of the media in people's lives.
   C. validity of expert opinions.
   D. comparing two ages of media reporting.
   E. different ways a story can be reported.

7. The author of Passage 2 would probably consider the last sentence of Passage 1 to be
   A. optimistic but misleading.
   B. unnecessarily grim.
   C. too vague to verify or discredit.
   D. pretentious and snobby.
   E. unusually perceptive.

8. Compared to the tone of Passage 1, the tone of Passage 2 is more
   A. scholarly.   D. conversational.
   B. apologetic.   E. somber.
   C. sentimental.

9. The last line of Passage 2 suggests that the author of Passage 1 has

   A. considered all the evidence carefully.

   B. failed to recognize public tastes and appetites.

   C. used a tone of voice that misses the point.

   D. lost touch with marketplace realities.

   E. faked the evidence.

Questions 10–18 are based on this passage:

The following excerpt is taken from the short story "I Went Back to Mars" by Michael Kabel:

I'd saved for months but the best passage I could afford went only so far as the supply station above Meroe Patera, a dilapidated wagon-wheel model from two (5)hundred years ago that was, incredibly, still in use. Stepping off the liner and through its airlock was like walking back in time: the scrubbed air might as well have twinkled with the dust that floated in (10)real sunlight back home.

Commuter shuttles, the ticket agent back home had promised me, left for the surface every two hours. A terminal at the farthest end of one spoke told me the (15)schedule had been cut back to twice daily, even going so far as to blame the economic troubles on the system-wide recession. I went back to the station's central hub, and the ring of calling booths (20)at its center. At one time the area might've looked like an urban plaza or seaside park. Now the plastic flower boxes were empty and the trees had dropped dead leaves to the ceramic floor.

(25)Of all the old names, only Halbursham still had a listed number. He broke out in a grin as his face came on the screen.

"Well, well, well," he said laughing. (30)"How you been, Johnny?"

His smile faded when I told him where I was. "You're really in orbit?"

I poked at the screen. On his end, it would look like I was trying to tap his (35)forehead. "I can't really explain right now," I said. "This thing's expensive."

"Of course." He glanced at something off to one side. "There's a cargo truck coming up in a bit. I'll set you up to hitch (40)a ride."

Two hours later the truck's pilot strapped me into a rear cockpit couch and fired the maneuvering jets. The station fell away from us, the craft rotating towards (45)the murky red and blue swirls of Mars. As we turned, I remembered my childhood fear of elevators and closed my eyes, dreading the sensation of waiting for a halt that never comes. At the end of the (50)drop I would imagine landing on springs, or steel cables above me pulling taut. So I wasn't paying attention as we descended towards the dark soil of the Elysium Plain.

(55)Halbursham waited for me on the runway, fatter since I'd been gone and with deep rings around his eyes smudged with red dust.

We hugged just like old friends. (60)"What have you been doing with yourself?" he asked.

"I'm a security analyst back on Earth," I said, trying to sound proud of myself. "At the space museum in New (65)New Orleans."

"I know what you're doing here," he said. "You've come back for Kyla, haven't you?"

I looked away. There were rain clouds **(70)**above the volcanic rills to the east. "The court's agreed to a hearing."

"The hell with them," he asked. "How did you persuade her mother?"

It had taken months to even get my **(75)**ex-wife to respond to my letters. "She wouldn't pass this up."

Halbursham led me to the motor pool and put a key fob in my hand. "Follow the old railroad, out to the Syrtis valleys," he **(80)**said. "You can't miss her husband's place."

When I tried to thank him, he walked off. "Best of luck to you, John." he said.

I called Lyssa from the phone inside **(85)**the dirty spaceport. Her new husband answered the phone.

"She took Kyla out for a walk," he said before I'd spoken. His face had the pinkish hue that is a kind of tan there, and **(90)**his hair was neatly combed despite the winds. "They'll be back within the half-hour."

I told him I'd be stopping by before heading on to a hotel in Kennedy City.

(95)"You're welcome to stay with us," he said calmly. "You've come a long way and it's stupid to run back and forth after that."

The kindness made me think before **(100)**speaking. "Thanks just the same."

Halbursham insisted on loaning me a jeep, a fairly new model with tires threaded like a screw. At the gates a throng of squatters milled about, their **(105)**shoulders stooped and their backs hunched, almost certainly from working off their emigration passage in some ore foundry under one of the mountains. Entire families stood or huddled against **(110)**the fence, some not taking their eyes off the sky to notice the jeep coming within inches of running them down. They were still looking up as I turned onto the highway, hypnotized by their own hopes **(115)**of escape floating out in the ruddy sky.

10. In line 4, "dilapidated" most nearly means
   A. brand-new.   D. rundown.
   B. innocent.   E. innovative.
   C. poorly built.

11. In lines 47–49, the description of elevators serves to
   A. show us the narrator is at heart a coward.
   B. show that the narrator doesn't want to crash.
   C. remind us the narrator is on another planet.
   D. foreshadow that Mars is a happy place.
   E. provide a real-world comparison to an interplanetary landing.

12. The author's main point in describing the space station is to show that
   A. the future will be an exciting time.
   B. not everything in the future will always be brand new.
   C. Mars is a very hostile planet.
   D. the narrator doesn't want to be there.
   E. not everyone wants to explore Mars.

13. The description of Lyssa's new husband in lines 85–96 includes what literary devices?
   A. foreshadowing and irony
   B. assertion and argument
   C. imagery and contrast
   D. dialogue and comparison
   E. invocation and definition

14. It can be inferred that since leaving Mars, the narrator

- A. has struggled with money and a new career.
- B. has kept close ties with old friends and family.
- C. wants to stay on Earth.
- D. has gotten rich.
- E. forgot why he left in the first place.

15. The expression "shoulders stooped" in line 105 conveys the degree to which

- A. people feel optimistic about getting on a spaceship.
- B. they hurry to get out of the narrator's way.
- C. they've had to endure hard labor since coming to Mars.
- D. no one wants to leave Mars.
- E. the people feel powerless to get inside the spaceport.

16. The narrator makes a long journey to a place from which many people are trying to get away. This is an example of

- A. imagery.
- B. irony.
- C. simile.
- D. metaphor.
- E. personification.

17. From the information provided in the passage, all of the following can be inferred about the Martian colonies EXCEPT

- A. people felt cheated after getting to Mars.
- B. people came to Mars wanting a better life.
- C. the colonies were once in better economic shape.
- D. life on Mars is hard and uncompromising.
- E. conditions on Mars will eventually get better.

Each sentence below has one or two blanks, each blank indicating that something has been omitted. Beneath the sentence are five choices, labeled A through E. Choose the word or combination of words that, when placed in the sentence, *best* fits the sentence's meaning.

---

18. The building inspector was in a hurry; he only gave the structure a _____ inspection.

- A. precipitous
- B. surreptitious
- C. perfunctory
- D. extraneous
- E. speculative

19. For scientists, _____ race to an ancient skill is misguided, in part because race isn't a scientific way to _____ human beings.

- A. acknowledging… recognize
- B. attributing… categorize
- C. describing… symbolize
- D. compelling… reconstruct
- E. enticing… classify

20. The exact reason for the disappearance of the dinosaurs remains a(n) _____ to this day.

   A.   augmentation   D.   enigma

   B.   simplicity   E.   adulteration

   C.   expiation

21. The explosion _____ into the island, ejecting thousands of tons of granite, igneous rock, and sediment.

   A.   eased   D.   arose

   B.   slammed   E.   bloomed

   C.   dropped

22. The reformer _____ change might ever come in a government _____ by hardline traditionalists.

   A.   doubted… dominated

   B.   believed… destroyed

   C.   insisted… detested

   D.   hoped… fraternized

   E.   stipulated… evacuated

23. Humpback whales are wondrous creatures—even their more _____ qualities have something _____ about them.

   A.   elaborate… boring

   B.   fantastic… affectionate

   C.   ordinary… fantastic

   D.   intelligent… cynical

   E.   human… mystical

Section III

20 Questions

Time – 20 Minutes

Questions 1–8 are based on the following passage:

Political campaigning can be difficult at times because the candidates usually have different views and opinions on a wide array of issues and agendas that (5)affect the overall running of the government. Campaigns can become particularly rough when candidates resort to tactics designed to undermine their opponent(s).

(10)This is called *negative campaigning*. Name calling and mudslinging are two types. Name calling is offensive and rude, whether on the playground or in a national campaign. (15)Unfortunately, candidates use it because it is direct, personal, and hard to disprove. *Mudslinging* is an expanded form of name calling, involving general accusations against each other that are (20)exaggerated and mean-spirited; for example, that the opponent never keeps promises; that one cannot trust his voting record; that he has always been a friend to special interest groups, etc.

(25)Unfortunately, using negative campaigning to get the most votes seems to benefit campaigns, though at times voters seem angry about the constant bickering and insults. The chance (30)that rudeness and outright deceit may help a campaign encourages candidates and their supporters "to keep using negativity." Citizens need to let candidates know what the limits of negative (35)campaigns should be.

Another element of negative campaigning is the *fear factor*. The term *bandwagon* refers to a candidate's persuading the voters by saying "Everybody's doing **(40)**it, so it must be right." This method of persuasion may work since some people fear being "left out of the crowd" or "out of step with their peers."

Politicians may use more positive **(45)**ways to sway the voters to their side by means such as using testimonials, glittering generalities, and the "Just Plain Folks" approach. A *testimonial* is a statement supporting a particular **(50)**candidate. It also helps if a well-liked politician or famous person endorses or gives testimony. *Endorsement* means to give support and approval of a candidate's qualifications and character. **(55)**Of course, the politician who endorses another candidate is not an opponent but rather someone who agrees with the candidate's political stand. The political endorser also believes that if the candidate **(60)**were elected, it would be beneficial to his or her cause or political party. Candidates may also try to use their ability to seem like plain folk, appealing to voters by voicing concerns about ordinary, **(65)**day-to-day struggles.

Another campaign tactic, *card stacking*, can be used in both a positive and negative way. Card stacking means citing data that has been carefully selected to **(70)**present only the best facts or worst facts about a situation.

Other methods used by candidates to try to win voter support are to address the current concerns of the *majority*. These **(75)**issues might be, for example, immigration quotas, environmental protection, or continuing affirmative action. Immigration quotas would be either a leniency towards immigration or a tougher **(80)**restriction placed upon how many people are allowed to enter the United States. Right to property and environmental protection issues might be concerns for a property owner wanting to **(85)**sell off a large tract of land to developers of a shopping mall. A conflict may occur if the public or a public agency tries to stop the development because it is building over the scarcity of wetlands in **(90)**that area and will affect the surrounding environment and ecosystem. Affirmative action is sometimes a topic of debate when members of a minority group feel discriminated against and feel that certain **(95)**special employment, housing, or educational opportunities should be granted them as compensation for past inequalities.

Some campaigns can be run so **(100)**successfully, utilizing the various techniques discussed in this section, that a candidate may develop a leading edge over an opponent. Voters may even transfer their alliance or association with **(105)**one candidate or political party to the other side. Opinions and feelings towards candidates can change during the campaigning process, which is why having a good campaign strategy is so **(110)**important to help win an election. There may be occasions when the best candidate for the job does not win the election in part because his or her campaign may not have been run as well **(115)**as an opponent's.

1. The author's primary purpose in this passage is to

   A. argue for reform in the political campaign system.

   B. defend some tactics political candidates make before an election.

   C. explain how positive campaigning almost never works.

   D. list and explain some types of negative campaigning.

   E. show why political campaigns often appeal only to the majority.

2. The first paragraph of this passage serves to

   A. provide a history of political campaigning in America.

   B. challenge conventional opinion about political campaigning.

   C. explain why some campaigns can turn negative.

   D. assert that candidates cannot stick to the issues.

   E. propose a new way of campaigning.

3. The phrase "left out of the crowd" in line 42 most closely means

   A. existing outside of popular behavior.

   B. shunned from one's peers and neighbors.

   C. forming one's own political party.

   D. hoping to become a socially popular.

   E. not aware of current trends.

4. According to the passage, which of the following is true about political endorsements?

   A. not everyone will believe an endorsement

   B. they can add glamour and excitement to a campaign

   C. they most often backfire

   D. not every candidate agrees to use them

   E. no one is fooled by them

5. The word "compensation" in line 97 most closely means

   A. payment for work done.

   B. to feel sorry for.

   C. a loan against future earnings.

   D. the race political candidates run.

   E. rewards to make up for a past injustice.

6. It can be inferred from the last paragraph that

   A. negative campaigning will soon be a thing of the past.

   B. not every candidate will use negative campaigning.

   C. affirmative action is wrong.

   D. negative campaigning will likely not go away.

   E. candidates enjoy negative campaigning.

7. An example of a testimonial would be

   A. a celebrity appearing at a campaign fundraiser.

   B. television ads attacking an opponent.

   C. the candidate offering thoughts on an issue.

   D. a private citizen saying the candidate helped him in the past.

   E. striking back at an opponent's own negative campaign.

8. The "rudeness and outright deceit" refers in this instance to

   A. the tactics of negative campaigning.

   B. way that political candidates behave personally.

   C. the problems with modern elections.

   D. poor standards of political endorsements.

   E. voter behavior at the polls.

Questions 9–20 are based on these passages:

The following passages consider the ways movies reflected popular moods at two points in the 20th century. The first relates to movies in the 1930s; the second, movies in the 1970s.

Passage 1:

By the height of the Great Depression in 1933, more Americans were flocking to movies than ever before, eager to escape the crushing poverty and pervading sense (5)of hopelessness that massive unemployment and growing debt brought on a seemingly daily basis. Because tickets cost only pennies and offered hours of diversion, they existed for millions of (10)Americans as a cheap way to fill the hours of the day. Moreover, movies had yet to escape the public perception as a "working class" medium—fit not for the cultured, educated elite but for the lower, (15)blue collar citizen and people of little, if any, secondary or high school education. Hollywood responded by making films that both appealed to peoples' yearnings for release from (20)economic want and attacked the government and social systems that produced the economic collapse which caused the Depression.

A great example of the films that both (25)exploited and glamorized a sense of financial security were the hugely popular "Thin Man" series starring William Powell and Myrna Loy as Nick and Nora Charles, rich socialites who (30)solved murders among New York's elite society. Set in luxurious wardrooms and expensive nightclubs, the murders always revolved around the idle rich and were motivated by petty emotions of (35)greed and vanity. Powell's Nick, a former working class gumshoe, uses common sense logic and a "from the streets" attitude to see through the affectations and snobbery of the socialites. In every (40)example, his unpretentious common sense won out over the idle rich's treachery, standing up for justice regardless of economic station.

Similarly, the "gangster" films that (45)first became prominent during this period showed audiences the modern-day outlaws of that era, individuals who defied the systems responsible for the Depression and made their own way in an uncaring (50)environment. Films such as *The Public Enemy* and *Angels with Dirty Faces* showed working class men and women clawing their way into riches despite the police and judges who stood in their way (55)—representatives of the same systems that many working class people held responsible for the Depression. That the criminals died violent, untimely deaths was almost beside the point to the (60)audiences who devoured these films; the gangster heroes won out, no matter the cost.

Passage 2:

By the 1970s, anxiety regarding the nation's direction and sense of identity (65)became reflected in popular entertainment, as a new generation of writers and directors—products of the social conscience of the previous decade —exerted their influence on the (70)entertainment mainstream. In the aftermath of the Vietnam War and the growing Watergate scandal, American film audiences entered into a renewed romance with the Western genre, albeit a (75)new strain that served as social allegory. In these New Westerns, the heroes were frequently lawbreakers and outcasts who rejected social convention and morality in order to make a life for (80)themselves on the American Frontier. Films such as *Butch Cassidy and the Sundance Kid* and *Jeremiah Johnson* (both starring Robert Redford) resonated deeply with audiences worried (85)about confining government and technological structures; *The Outlaw Josie Wales*, about a Confederate solider (Clint Eastwood) looking to lead a productive life in the West, spoke to the post-(90)Vietnam yearning for individual redemption. Similarly, the brutal violence of vigilante films such as *Dirty Harry* (also with Eastwood) and *Taxi Driver* enthralled audiences beleaguered by skyrocketing crime rates and a weakened justice system. In both types of films, the **(95)**recurring theme is "don't trust the governments or economies; you're on your own." The theme continued throughout the decade, spiraling into urban political drama (*Serpico*), science **(100)**fiction (*The Omega Man*), and even romance (*Love Story*). While by the beginnings of the 1980s the pessimism had thawed somewhat, the 1970s spirit of individualism influenced the next **(105)**generation of filmmakers who came of age in the 1990s, crafting such anti-establishment works as *The Shawshank Redemption*, *Traffic* and *The Matrix*.

9. Which of the following is an overarching theme of both passages?

    A. Movies remained violent for 60 years.
    B. Movies both reflect and comfort the social anxieties of their audience.
    C. People are drawn to violent movies more than less violent movies.
    D. Filmmakers of the 1990s were influenced by films of the 1930s.
    E. Poor people only like violent movies.

10. The sentence beginning "That the criminals died…" (lines 57–58) indicates that

    A. people continued to cheer for movie gangsters, despite the films' morals.
    B. people realized gangsters were bad.
    C. gangsters lived on after their deaths.
    D. moviegoers wanted to be gangsters.
    E. authorities insisted movie gangsters die at movie's end.

11. In line 103, "thawed" most nearly means

    A. remained cynical.
    B. fell deeply in love.
    C. quickly become soured.
    D. slowly got worse.
    E. slowly became more positive.

12. In Passage 1, the author's attitude towards the gangster movies is one of

    A. open affection.
    B. objective curiosity.
    C. distanced consideration.
    D. measured disdain.
    E. vague worry.

13. In line 53, "clawing" most nearly means

    A. lazing.
    B. using fingernails.
    C. swiping at.
    D. struggling.
    E. hoping.

14. It can be inferred from the first paragraph that the author

    A. doesn't care about the opinions of police and lawmakers.
    B. believes that rich people didn't normally attend movies in the 1930s.
    C. believes gangster movies superior to other types of movies.
    D. wants to be a filmmaker.
    E. has never seen a gangster film.

15. Compared to the author of Passage 1, the author of Passage 2 shows a greater concern about the

A. number of movies being released.

B. limited availability of movies dealing with social concerns.

C. problems faced by people in a given decade.

D. creation of dialogue between filmgoers and moviemakers.

E. individual's response to movies' treatments of social themes.

16. The author of Passage 1 links the popularity of gangster films primarily with

A. public eagerness to see violence onscreen.

B. the public's hunger to see individuals revolt against the social system.

C. new advances in movie technology.

D. public outrage about police incompetence.

E. a rise in the crime rate.

17. The statement in lines 94–95 ("don't trust the governments or…") primarily indicates the author of Passage 2 believes that

A. films of the 1970s offered a deep suspicion of society.

B. filmmakers were too obsessed with "message" in their movies.

C. films of the 1970s weren't socially conscious enough.

D. films of the 1970s were socially conscious to a fault.

E. films have different messages for the viewer to assimilate.

18. What situation is reflected in the atmosphere of both decades discussed in the passages, according to their authors?

A. Films failed to reflect the society of their viewers.

B. Filmmakers forced their ideas on audiences.

C. Audiences welcomed their social concerns expressed on film.

D. Social concerns inspired audiences to request movies.

E. Studios had a political agenda in making crime films.

19. In line 45, the "modern-day outlaws" are considered to be

A. people that society finds reprehensible.

B. individuals working outside the social system.

C. cowboys in the Great Depression.

D. glorious heroes.

E. the politicians responsible for the Great Depression.

20. The author of Passage 1 would most likely view the vigilante films of the 1970s as

A. a passing fad.

B. part of a long tradition of social relevance in film.

C. the logical descendent of the gangster film.

D. A and B only.

E. B and C only.

Diagnostic Test Evaluation Chart			
	Diagnostic Test Questions		
Chapter	**Section I**	**Section II**	**Section III**
1 Author's Purpose and Attitude	10, 16, 23, 24	7, 8, 12	1, 2, 7, 8, 12, 15, 20
2 Sentence Completion	1, 2, 3, 4, 5, 6, 7, 8, 23	1, 2, 3, 4, 5, 10, 18, 19, 20, 21, 22, 23	5, 11, 13
3 Critical Reading	9, 11, 12, 13, 14, 15, 17, 18, 19, 20, 21, 22	6, 9, 10, 14, 17	3, 4, 6, 8, 10, 11, 13, 14, 15, 16, 17, 18, 19
4 Interpreting Literature		11, 12, 13, 15, 16, 17	9

SAT Preparation Resources

Among the resources that you may find helpful as you prepare for the SAT Reading Test (and the entire SAT) are the following:

CollegeBoard
www.collegeboard.com

This is an excellent site to review as you prepare. Click on "Prepare for the SAT" on the right-hand side of the main page. The SAT prep page offers a wealth of ways to prepare for the test, some free and some for purchase. In the left column, you can choose to take practice tests and find out more about each section of the test, including Critical Reading.

SparkNotes Test Prep: The New SAT
www.sparknotes.com/testprep/books/newsat/

This is a non-nonsense, step-by-step preparation guide. It offers insight into what you will see on the SAT and tips for what to do and not do as you study for and take the test.

Chapter 1
Author's Purpose and Attitude

The SAT Critical Reading section contains passages on a wide variety of topics. These topics are taken from social sciences (anthropology, history, sociology), the humanities (arts, culture, philosophy), natural sciences (earth science, biology, space exploration) and literature (creative fiction). The passages may be long (500–800 words) or short (around 100 words).

No matter the topic or length, each author had a purpose for writing: to inform, to entertain, to motivate, to persuade, or to achieve any other purpose. Understanding the author's purpose aids in understanding the passage and responding to questions.

After all, authors are people too, and they have their own ways of looking at ideas. This is called their **attitude**, and it can be biased, objective, or neutral. A biased attitude tends to see only one side of an issue. An objective attitude considers both sides of the issue equally, and a neutral attitude takes no stance at all but merely presents information. In SAT passages, if an author has a specific attitude, it is usually expressed as an **argument**, which is supported by **evidence**.

For the SAT Critical Reading section, it is important to determine both the author's purpose and attitude to provide you with the best perspective on the passage to answer the questions that follow it.

One of the most basic ways to determine an author's purpose and attitude is to learn to recognize the **organizational patterns** the author uses in order to accomplish his or her purpose. Another important skill in determining purpose and attitude is the ability to recognize the author's **tone**.

PURPOSE

An author will rarely state the purpose of writing a passage: it has to be *inferred* from the information in the passage and from the way in which that information is presented. For instance, if the author's main purpose for writing about how the great pyramids were built is simply to inform, that passage will almost exclusively contain facts. Very few *qualitative* words, such as "unbelievable," "greatest," or "inspiring," will appear in the text.

In SAT passages, the author's purpose must be identified through careful reading. One guideline, however, is that few passages are purely **narrative** in style (that is, they exist only to tell a story or entertain the reader). The passages, especially those about social science and natural science subjects, are almost always **persuasive** (wanting to convince the reader of an opinion's validity) or **expository** (instructing the reader or relating a series of events). Be advised that you may encounter a **literary passage**, taken from a work of fiction or nonfiction. Examples of these less-frequent passage types will be discussed in Chapter 4.

Although persuasive and expository passages may be written to "persuade" or "instruct," these terms on their own are too simplistic for the SAT. Test questions will, instead, require a deeper understanding of exactly what the persuasion or instruction is about. More specific descriptions of purposes might include the following:

- **to discuss** the benefits of space exploration for science
- **to describe** the motivations of archeologists in solving the mysteries of buried civilizations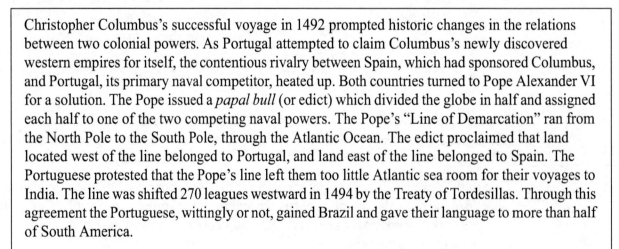
- **to reveal** the suffering that immigrants undergo in search of freedom
- **to illustrate** the relationship between manicured lawns and groundwater pollution
- **to provide evidence of** the effects of land development on Native American cultures
- **to explain** how music is marketed in an exclusive system

Read the following two practice passages, and answer the questions regarding the purpose of each.

Christopher Columbus's successful voyage in 1492 prompted historic changes in the relations between two colonial powers. As Portugal attempted to claim Columbus's newly discovered western empires for itself, the contentious rivalry between Spain, which had sponsored Columbus, and Portugal, its primary naval competitor, heated up. Both countries turned to Pope Alexander VI for a solution. The Pope issued a *papal bull* (or edict) which divided the globe in half and assigned each half to one of the two competing naval powers. The Pope's "Line of Demarcation" ran from the North Pole to the South Pole, through the Atlantic Ocean. The edict proclaimed that land located west of the line belonged to Portugal, and land east of the line belonged to Spain. The Portuguese protested that the Pope's line left them too little Atlantic sea room for their voyages to India. The line was shifted 270 leagues westward in 1494 by the Treaty of Tordesillas. Through this agreement the Portuguese, wittingly or not, gained Brazil and gave their language to more than half of South America.

The primary purpose of this passage is

- A. to instruct readers on the making of maps in the fifteenth century.
- B. to describe the power of papal bulls.
- C. to relate the effects of the Spain/Portugal rivalry on exploration.
- D. to inform readers about one effect of Columbus's voyage.
- E. to persuade the reader of the effectiveness of the Pope in solving international problems.

Although all answers reflect a true statement about the passage, the correct answer is **D**. If you reread the question, you will note that it asks about the ***primary*** purpose of the passage. A passage may serve more than one purpose, but it usually has only one primary purpose. This purpose is not described in answer **A,** because the passage was not particularly about how maps, in general, were made in the fifteenth century. The answer **B** is also not precise enough. The effect of one particular papal bull is discussed in the passage, but papal bulls and their influence are not directly discussed. Answer **E** states that the purpose is to persuade, yet no judgment or evaluation of events is made within the passage, only facts are given. Only Columbus's voyage is discussed in the context of that rivalry. As for answer **C**, there may have been numerous effects of the Spain/Portugal rivalry, but they are not addressed in this passage. Therefore, answer **D** is correct.

This passage was written by a judge in the Salem Witch Trials of 1692, in Salem, Massachusetts

About Midsummer, in the year 1688, the Eldest of these Children, who is a Daughter, saw cause to examine their Washerwoman, upon their missing of some Linen' [linens] which ·twas fear'd she had stollen from them; and of what use this linnen might be to serve the Witchcraft intended, the Theef's Tempter knows! This Laundress was the Daughter of an ignorant and a scandalous old Woman in the Neighbourhood; whose miserable Husband before he died, had sometimes complained of her, that she was undoubtedly a Witch, and that whenever his Head was laid, she would quickly arrive unto the punishments due to such an one. This Woman in her daughters Defence bestow'd very bad Language upon the Girl that put her to the Question; immediately upon which, the poor child became variously indisposed in her health, and visited with strange Fits, beyond those that attend an Epilepsy or a Catalepsy, or those that they call The Diseases of Astonishment.

This passage serves mainly to

A.   introduce the reader to an unusual character in the community.

B.   to teach readers about the typical behavior of witches.

C.   to convince the reader that there was good cause to suspect the woman of being a witch.

D.   to name the husband of the Washerwoman as a chief witness in her guilt.

E.   to describe an example of a witch's language upon a girl who had challenged her behavior.

Answers **A**, **B**, **D**, and **E** state information which occurs in the text. However, they do not reflect the text's main purpose. Remember, as the italicized writing at the top of the passage states, the writer of this text was a judge at a historical witch trial. Throughout the text, the writer **insinuates** (or hints at) several examples of strangeness and inexplicable powers in the woman he is writing about. By doing so, he is apparently trying to convince the reader that there is cause to suspect the woman of being a witch. Answer **C** is correct.

TIP

The second passage above shows the importance of *reading the italicized information before most SAT reading passages*. It conveys hints about the author's purpose.

Practice 1: Author's Purpose

Read the following passages and answer the question that follows each.

Passage 1

The framers of the U.S. Constitution had a critical choice to make. They had set up a modern democracy, generally based on the ancient Greek system and reinforced with the philosophies of European thinkers. They were placing tremendous responsibility into the hands of the common citizen. The country could stand or fall depending on the integrity of the electoral procedure, particularly in regards to electing the president and the vice president.

These architects of democracy knew they could not leave such a decision to the Congress. The inequality of numbers in that branch of government would not ensure an equal voice to all states. Yet, could they trust a largely uneducated and superstitious populace to choose the best leader? They recognized that simple majority rule often equated to "mob rule."

ALEXANDER HAMILTON

The solution, written by Alexander Hamilton, came in the form of a compromise called the Electoral College and was written into the Constitution. It called for a system by which each state would cast votes for a number of "electors" that would equal the sum of their senators and representatives. Electors would then cast votes for two out of a list of candidates. These electoral votes would then be counted during a joint session of Congress. The top two choices would become the president and the vice president.

From Hamilton's time until today, there has been a critical change in this process. Today, electors vote according to the popular votes of their states. For instance, if most of the voters from Maine voted for Candidate A, the Maine electors will vote for Candidate A. In Jefferson's time, the voters would basically vote for electors, who would then vote according to their own wills.

1. This passage was written primarily to

    A. acknowledge a critical contribution by Alexander Hamilton to American politics.
    B. explain the origin of the electoral college and compare it with today's process.
    C. defend the validity of the electoral process in America.
    D. argue for the superiority of today's electoral process over the original.
    E. prove that "mob rule" is the lowest form of democracy.

Passage 2

Most students are acquainted with some of the more crucial landmark Supreme Court decisions. *Plessy v. Ferguson* established the segregationist framework referred to as "separate but equal" in 1896. This ruling mandated that blacks and whites could live separately and avoid, under penalty of law, any social intermingling. Over a half century later, *Brown v. Board of Education of Topeka, KS* overturned that social regime.

Perhaps far fewer students are aware of a somewhat less celebrated case called *Dorothy E. Davis, et al. v. County School Board of Prince Edward County, VA*. Yet this case, along with three similar cases, was part of the U.S. Supreme Court's *Brown* ruling in 1954. *Dorothy E. Davis* began when the students of Robert Russa Moton High School in Farmville went on strike to protest the lack of facilities, space, and funds in their segregated high school. The purpose of the strike was to draw attention to the discrepancy between their school and a neighboring all-white school, which had well-appointed facilities and well-paid teachers.

For all their initiative and courage, young students cannot always change the attitudes of a school board by themselves. The Moton High School students asked for the support of the NAACP. They received it in the form of a federal lawsuit against the school board to end discrimination. It was a huge challenge, but *Dorothy E. Davis v. County School Board of Prince Edward County, VA* went all the way to the highest court in the land. As part of the *Brown* case, which the Supreme Court was also deciding at the time, *Dorothy E. Davis* became part of the overturning of *Plessy v. Ferguson*, and the demise of segregation in America.

2. The primary purpose of this passage is

   A. to denounce the "separate but equal" directive.
   B. to catalog the history of the fall of segregation in America.
   C. to relate a lesser-known subplot in the history of desegregation.
   D. to commend the courage of high school students who take the lead.
   E. to argue against discrimination in a free society.

Passage 3

The rate of population growth is measured by using a mathematical formula which notes the change in population numbers per a period of time. The equation looks like this:

$$dN/dt = rN$$

The lower case *d* means "change in." The capital *N* stands for the present population number. The *t* means time. Finally, the lower case *r* stands for the rate of population growth. In other words, the rate of population growth equals the change in the population numbers per a given period of time.

The *r* factor represents the average number of offspring each individual in the population contributes to population growth. If each individual on average had one offspring, *r* would equal 1, and there would be no population growth. If *r* = 2, the population would double. And so on.

Applying this formula to the lower trophic level species such as fish, which produce abundant offspring, the average number of offspring produced by each individual would be high, possibly in the hundreds. Therefore, the overall population growth (*rN*) would be high. On the other hand, species on a higher trophic level, such as horses, might have an *r* factor of only 1.3. That means that each horse may produce 1.3 horses over the given

period of time—on average, of course! In this case, the overall population of horses would obviously increase at a lower rate than that of fish.

Through understanding the significance of each factor of the formula, one can see that it can be roughly translated as "the growth of the population is a function of the population growth contribution of each individual over a period of time." Looking closely at this statement, one can deduce the role of the intervention in population growth. Take the *dt* factor. The passage of time cannot be controlled. It cannot be slowed down or sped up, at least within our four-dimensional existence. Therefore, the part of the formula that can be varied is *r*. If the rate of individual reproduction is increased or decreased, then *dN* — the change in population — can be controlled.

3. This passage was written primarily to

   A. show that manipulating population growth hinges on controlling individual contribution.
   B. illustrate the difference between species of higher and lower trophic levels.
   C. explain how population numbers are increased over time.
   D. convince the reader that it is imperative to control population growth in certain species.
   E. argue for the intervention of scientists in the population growth of lower trophic species.

ORGANIZATIONAL PATTERNS AND THE AUTHOR'S PURPOSE

Authors may use different **organizational patterns** to achieve different purposes. These include patterns and techniques you may have learned to use in writing yourself, so you may recognize them in the following lists. These lists include some, though not all, of the possible patterns and techniques an author can employ.

Organizational Patterns	Possible Purpose
Cause-effect	Inform, convince
Problem-solution	Convince, call to action
Contrasting ideas	Analyze, inform, possibly conclude
Chronological order	Inform, often historical information
Order of importance	Outline procedures, suggest solutions
Information/analysis	Build an argument, draw a conclusion

EXAMPLES OF ORGANIZATIONAL PATTERNS AND AUTHOR'S PURPOSE

- **Cause-Effect**: A passage on the pollution of waterways and the mutation of frogs. Informs about causes, traces the links between those causes and the resultant problems. May draw a conclusion on the need for change

- **Problem-Solution**: A passage on motor vehicle accidents as number-one killer of teens. Convinces with information on statistics and specific cases; calls to action by recommending ways to minimize the factors which lead to teen motor vehicle accidents

- **Comparing or contrasting ideas**: A passage explaining the differences and similarities between private and public colleges. Informs of options, may analyze benefits and drawbacks, may conclude regarding preferability

- **Order of Importance**: A passage on how to administer CPR. Informs of procedure, prioritizes order of action

- **Information/Analysis, also called Statement/Support**: A passage stating that economic conditions are forcing some Latin Americans to resort to life-threatening measures to immigrate to the United States. Supports statement with examples, illustrations, description, statistics or other forms of evidence.

By becoming familiar with the various forms of organizing information, you can quickly identify an author's purpose.

Practice 2: Organization Patterns and the Author's Purpose

A. Read each of the following passages, and then answer the questions that follow.

Passage 1

Throughout the world, extraordinary achievements in architecture stand as monuments not only to the purposes to which the builder ascribed them, but also to the exalted levels of potential human brilliance and inspiration. Two such structures are the Taj Mahal in India and St. Basil's Cathedral in Russia.

Rising almost mystically out of the surroundings of the city of Agra, the Taj Mahal, built entirely of pure white marble, seems to glow with radiance. The structure consists of four tall minarets that stand sentry-like around the main building, all in front of a long, serene reflecting pool.

In the mid 17th century, the emperor Shah Jahan ordered the Taj Mahal built in remembrance of his beloved wife, Mumtaz Mahal, who had died in childbirth. The main building houses Mumtaz's tomb. Next to it, and less ornate, lies her husband's tomb. Every inch of the spacious walls of the building is decorated with floral-like patterns consisting of inlaid colorful precious stones. The roof of the building tapers into an elegant dome shape, reflecting the traditional style of Mogul Islamic

TAJ MAHAL

architecture. The tapering, pointed dome of the mausoleum may have inspired the great poet Rabindranath Tagore to describe the edifice as "a teardrop.... on the face of time."

Almost exactly a century before the building of the Taj Mahal, Ivan the Terrible, Tsar of Russia, ordered a similarly immortal structure to be built on Red Square in Moscow. A celebration of victory at war, St. Basil's Cathedral consists of eight vividly painted chapels surrounding a ninth chapel which houses the tomb of St. Basil. Each chapel is crowned with a magnificent, onion-shaped dome. Inside the chapels the space is cramped and dimly lit. Walls are covered with graceful stylized multi-color floral designs.

True to his fiercesome reputation, Ivan attempted to establish the eternal uniqueness of his monument through brutal means. After the completion of the cathedral, he ordered its architect, Postnik Yakovlev, to be blinded. His rationale was that the artist would thereby be disabled from producing another such masterpiece.

Two structures, one built by a lover, one by a warrior, both unparalleled in history, speak to the extremes of human passion and represent the heights of human artistry.

ST. BASIL'S CATHEDRAL

1. This passage was written primarily to

    A. guide travelers to two of the greatest architectural attractions in the world.

    B. trace the history of European and Islamic architecture.

    C. convince the reader that the Taj Mahal and St. Basil's Cathedral are the two finest architectural accomplishments in the world.

    D. describe two architectural masterpieces from a similar era.

    E. illustrate how great architecture comes from great leaders.

2. The organizational pattern this passage uses is

    A. cause and effect.   C. statement and support.   E. chronological order.

    B. comparing ideas.   D. order of ideas.

Passage 2

The following passage is an excerpt from an address to the people of the United States by the Council of the Cherokee Nation, in 1830.

We wish to remain on the land of our fathers. We have a perfect and original right to claim this, without interruption or molestation. The treaties with us... guarantee our residence, and our privileges, and secure us against intruders. Our only request is that these treaties may be fulfilled, and these laws executed.

But if we are compelled to leave our country, we see nothing but ruin before us. The country west of the Arkansas territory is unknown to us. From what we can learn of it, we have no prepossessions in its favor. All the inviting parts of it, as we believe, are preoccupied by various Indian nations, to which it has been assigned. They would regard us as intruders, and look upon us with an evil eye. The far greater part of that region is, beyond all controversy, badly supplied with wood and water; and no Indian tribe can live as agriculturists without these articles. All our neighbors, in case of our removal, though crowded into our near vicinity, would speak a language totally different from ours, and practice different customs.

The original possessors of that region are now wandering savages lurking for prey in the neighborhood. They have always been at war, and would be easily tempted to turn their arms against peaceful immigrants. Were the country to which we are urged much better than it is represented to be and were it free from the objections which we have made to it, still it is not the land of our birth, nor of our affections. It contains neither the scenes of our childhood, nor the graves of our fathers.

3. The primary purpose of this passage is

    A.   to point out to the US government the injustice of removing Indians from their lands.
    B.   to find an alternative solution to banishing the Cherokee from their lands.
    C.   to provide reasons why the Cherokee did not want to leave their land.
    D.   to blame the people of the United States for the suffering of the Cherokee.
    E.   to argue that the United States government should have given better land to the Cherokee.

4. The organizational pattern of this passage can best be described as

    A.   information/analysis.   C.   order of importance.   E.   information/analysis.
    B.   compare and contrast.   D.   problem/solution.

AUTHOR'S ATTITUDE

An author's **attitude** is the author's perspective, or feeling, about a topic. This attitude may be **objective**, based primarily on fact; or it can be **biased**, based primarily on opinion. An author writes from an objective attitude when the main purpose of the passage is to inform with facts. For example, a passage on the process of smelting, (releasing metals from ore), would most likely be comprised of facts and written objectively. An author writes from a biased attitude when the main purpose of the passage is to express opinion. For example, a passage on the effects of mining and smelting ore and the insufficient attention these effects may be given by mining companies might contain facts that supported the author's attitude and opinion that the metal workers needed better health benefits.

Most SAT passages are *not* straightforward, objective, fact-filled excerpts. Even information-based passages, with careful reading, will reveal an author's bias on the subject. Usually, this bias is not directly stated but implied. Read each passage thoroughly, looking for critical or judgmental words or phrases to determine the author's point of view.

INDIRECT BIAS

Authors do not always directly express their attitudes. Instead, they often present their bias **indirectly**, writing in a way that persuades the reader to adopt the author's opinion but does not openly state the bias itself. Indirect bias can be expressed by:

- Emphasizing information on one side of an issue
- Minimizing the importance of information on the other side of an issue
- Carefully choosing words that influence the reader to feel a certain way
- Choosing what information to include and what to ignore

All the above techniques are effective in portraying an author's bias in an indirect way. Most SAT passages, if they present a bias at all, present it in an indirect way.

The following are two passages on the same subject. One passage is objective and one has a biased attitude. Decide which passage is objective, and which is biased. What is the attitude of the biased passage? Then read the discussion that follows the two passages.

Passage 1

When settlers moved to the western American states in the 1800s, a large number of wildlife still roamed throughout the region. One of the most prevalent wild animals was the wolf, which enjoyed a wide distribution throughout North America above 15 degrees North Latitude. Wolves survive by hunting both small and large animals. They have been known to nourish themselves with mice and other rodents, while also being capable of bringing down a caribou or deer when necessary. The arrival of 19th century ranchers in the western states introduced a dietary option which appealed to the wolf population: domestic livestock.

Many of the ranchers who settled in the West came from Europe. For centuries, Europeans had perceived wolves to be evil and dangerous. For centuries, myth and superstition had infused European knowledge of this wild animal. Most of the settlers maintained these beliefs after their migration to America. As the resident wolf population turned their attention to the new supply of nourishment offered by the ranchers, relations between man and beast grew from distrustful to hostile. In the early 1900s, the federal government, at the ranchers' urging, began a program to regulate the wolf population in the ranchlands. Successful in its aim, the program eliminated sufficient numbers of the wolf to apprehend the threat to ranchers.

One of the species most severely effected by the wolf population control program was the gray wolf, which faced extinction by 1930. In 1995, steps were taken to bring the gray wolf back to the West. Wolves were brought in from Canada and the population began to grow. The project was so successful that in 2000 the ranches again began to feel threatened by the presence of this predator in their midst.

Passage 2

Ranchers in Montana, Idaho, and Wyoming have lived off the land and livestock for generations. Americans are fond of images of these cowboys rustling cattle and sheep through vast tracts of ranch land. An icon of the American spirit of independence, the cowboy has come to stand for freedom, romance, and adventure in American myth and legend. Americans rely on the meat produced by these ranchers for sustenance. Cowboy recreation such as rodeos, barn dancing, mounted shooting and bronco riding have become mainstays of American culture. The American image, both at home and abroad, has been significantly influenced by the spirit of the cowboy.

Yet these symbols of the American West are facing a threat. For decades, their states have been almost wolf-free. Lately, however, conservationists and wildlife scientists decided that wolves belonged in the wilds of these lands. In the 1990s, these activists transported sixty-six grey wolves from Alberta, Canada, to be released in Idaho. Those sixty-six have now grown to over three hundred in population. Wolves live by hunting. A pasture full of sheep or grasslands full of cattle are attractive to them. When farmers lose livestock, they lose money. When farmers lose livestock, the price of steak dinners increases. When a lifestyle of ranching is threatened, the very heart of the American image is pierced.

DISCUSSION

Passage 1 presents facts and information about the background of western ranchers and the history of wolves in their states. It does not express an opinion about the topic. Nor does it emphasize certain facts in order to make a point. It is an example of **objective** writing.

The second passage presents the writer's specific point of view. The author cites examples of how the presence of American western ranchers and cowboys have contributed immensely to the culture and image of America, both at home and throughout the world. The author also mentions the practical contributions cowboys have made to America, particularly food and recreational activities. Then the author presents a picture of these cowboys as being threatened by the deliberate introduction of wolves into their states. The reader, having followed the author's descriptions of the value of cowboys, will also see, through the author's eyes, the apparent injustice of this move by wildlife supporters. Therefore, in this passage, the author's attitude is **biased** towards supporting ranchers in their struggle against wolves.

ATTITUDE AND EVIDENCE

When a passage is objective and contains only information and facts, then no argument, opinion, or bias is presented in the passage. When the passage is written from a specific bias, it is, in effect, an argument. As you know from learning the principles of persuasive writing, all arguments require **evidence**. The SAT Critical Reading section contains many questions on evidence. These questions do not usually mention the word "evidence," but will often use "support." These questions are usually written in forms such as the following:

1. Which statement is supported by the example in the third paragraph?

2. Lines 31–38 support the idea that...

3. Which statement in the second paragraph supports the idea that...

To be prepared to answer questions about evidence, it is necessary to become practiced at identifying the author's bias, the argument presented, and the evidence cited to support the argument. As an example, take another look at the second passage in the section on wolves and ranchers. What is the author's bias? The author's bias is against wolves as threats to the American rancher. What is the author's argument? The argument is not directly stated, but a careful reading of the entire passage reveals a clear idea that wolves should not be supported as natural residents of American ranchlands. The argument goes as far as stating that a threat to American ranchers is a threat to all of America.

What is the evidence presented by the author? The first paragraph offers several ideas that support the author's argument:

- Ranchers are important to Americans, providing sources of food.
- Cowboys are important as symbols of the American spirit of independence.
- Cowboys have contributed many areas of entertainment to the American culture.
- The western cowboy has presented a romantic image of America throughout the world.

These statements are all evidence that the cowboy and the ranching lifestyle is crucial to America, both past and present, and both nationally and internationally. With this evidence, the author persuades the reader to accept the author's attitude and argument.

ATTITUDE, TONE, AND LANGUAGE

An author's attitude is revealed through his tone and language. If an author uses a respectful tone and complimentary language, it indicates a *positive* bias towards the subject. For instance, an author who is impressed by the work of cowboys may describe it is this way:

> "Days on the ranch can be long and boring or arduous and fast paced. They require men and women of great patience, perseverance, strength, and ingenuity."

On the other hand, a tone of disdain, condescension, or ridicule indicates a *negative* bias and will include language that is critical or derogatory.

> "The typical roundup today can boast less of the glamour Hollywood has endowed it with and more of the clamor of a dusty, dirty scene in which shouting men on hard-ridden horses treat cattle more like enemies than animals."

The tone of the first quote is obviously one of respect and admiration for the work of cattle owners. It characterizes ranch work as requiring some of the best qualities a worker can have. The tone and language of the second quote indicates a critical attitude. Words such as *clamor, glamour, dusty, dirty,* and *shouting* evoke a negative scene. The idea of cattle being treated as enemies rather than animals is critical and virtually equates cattle roundups with war.

In the SAT reading section, questions about the author's tone are sometimes stated like:

1. The author's tone can best be described as...

Other questions will ask you to infer what the author might think about another topic based on the author's expressed tone and attitude. These questions may be asked in this way:

2. The author would probably agree with which following statement?

While reading each passage, notice the language used and if it is critical or positive. Try to determine for yourself the author's tone. Then answer any question about tone by deciding which is closest to the author's tone.

Practice 3: Author's Attitude

Read the following two passages. Then answer the questions that follow.

Passage 1

The 341st Training Squadron, Lackland Air Force Base, San Antonio, Texas, is charged with the raising and training of Military Working Dogs (MWD). The MWD program's mission is to prepare selected breeds of dogs for active duty in military environments, including war zones. For this work, the choice of dogs suitable for training is highly selective. Two of the most common breeds used for this unique area of national defense are the German Shepherd and the Belgian Malinois. These breeds excel in intelligence, loyalty, trainability, and courage. Physically they also possess what no human troops can bring to the military: exceptional senses of smell and hearing.

The 341st Training Squadron provides the best MWD training in the world. Each year, approximately 400 dogs are put through their basic training at the base. About seventy-five percent of these dogs are trained as detector dogs, while one quarter are trained as patrol dogs specializing in search and attack duty. Detector dogs are trained to detect bombs and drugs. They are stationed at military installations around the world, and along national borders, where they are capable of uncovering a wide variety of drugs.

Currently 1,400 MWDs are serving with their highly skilled K-9 unit handlers throughout the world. But this quality of military service commands a price. The cost of running the training program is $420,000 per year. The cost of buying the dogs itself is considerable. Each year hundreds of dogs are hand selected by specialists who travel to Europe to purchase the best dogs available. Average price: $4,000 each. Weigh this expense against the number of American lives saved by MWDs and the amount of drug related crime averted since the program commenced after World War II. From this perspective, these dogs' contribution to national defense amounts to more than a dollar value.

1. The author's tone can be best described as

    A. critical.   B. respectful.   C. derisive.   D. neutral.   E. amused.

2. The author would probably agree with which following statement?

    A. The U.S. Department of Defense should decrease spending on the MWD program.

    B. The MWD program occupies a unique and moderately useful niche in the U.S. military.

    C. Expensive dogs are unfairly subjected to dangerous situations by the American military.

    D. The U.S. military exploits the ignorance of animals to the benefit of human soldiers.

    E. More American tax money to support the MWD program would be well placed.

Passage 2

Each year, Americans in increasing numbers flock to malls for entertainment, procurement of needed items, a break in the schedule, or whatever reason will suffice for the day. The average American spends over 6 hours shopping every week. Many people today consider shopping as a recreational activity. Over 90 percent of teenage girls consider store-hopping a favorite activity. Money seems to be of little consequence. Clothing items produced literally for pennies entice shoppers with hefty $100 price tags. Yet Americans are in more debt and have fewer savings today than ever before.

The pressure to dress in the latest fashions and to consume the latest products fuels a fire unknown to most who do not live according to those pressures, and that fire is a plight to laborers in developing countries around the world, who produce the clothes Americans buy. It is the conditions of people in dozens of countries like Indonesia, China, and Vietnam, who work from morning until night for wages insufficient to feed their families. It is the economic framework which facilitates impoverished countries to produce the goods that will sustain exceptionally high profits for businesses in developed countries.

Efforts have been made by international companies to mitigate the exploitation rampant in countries which have "sweatshop" working conditions. In 1997, the Clinton administration announced a new code of conduct for businesses with international product sources. This initiative, in agreement with business leaders, non-government agencies, church leaders, and human rights groups, called for a voluntary adherence to business practices which would limit child labor, control the length of the work week, and ensure that minimum wage was paid to all workers.

While the agreement was a step in a positive direction, it remains a voluntary policy. In some cases children under 15 can be put to work, and workers can work as many as 60 hours per week, as long as the worker "volunteers" to work the overtime. When the regular 48 hours of work each week fail to pay enough to subsist on, it is likely that the worker will have little choice but to "volunteer" to work several more hours at a paltry 12 to 60 cents per hour.

3. The author's tone can be best described as

   A. condescending.   C. hopeful.   E. neutral.

   B. ironic.   D. disapproving.

4. The statement in paragraph 1 that "over 90 percent of teenage girls consider store-hopping a favorite activity" supports the idea that

    A. Americans spend an average of 6 hours a week shopping.

    B. Americans commonly think of shopping as a recreational activity.

    C. Americans are more in debt today than ever before.

    D. money does not seem to be an issue for many American shoppers.

    E. human beings are exploited in developing countries for American merchandise.

5. The author's attitude in this passage is that

    A. all sweatshops are harmful for both developing countries and for Americans.

    B. initiatives against sweatshops that are not definitive and enforceable are useless.

    C. the use of sweatshops benefits the economies of the countries they exist in.

    D. the demand for new fashions feeds the economies of developing countries.

    E. Americans provide much needed jobs to developing countries through shopping.

CHAPTER 1 REVIEW

Passage 1

The Marquis de Lafayette

By the age of 13, Gilbert du Montier, a French nobleman known as the Marquis de Lafayette, was a wealthy orphan. Perhaps it was this sad, enforced independence early in life that gave him the spirit of a freedom fighter. Coming from a military family, the young Marquis studied at the French military academy and by age 16 had achieved the level of captain in the French cavalry. But in 1776, the spirit of revolution took hold of Lafayette when he heard of the Declaration of Independence, which had just been drafted across the ocean in America.

The young officer became deeply interested in the struggle for independence taking place in America. His heart was captured by the promise of liberty and freedom expressed by the American colonists, and service in France became insufficient to assuage his restless idealism. He, like many young Frenchmen of the time, was beginning to dream the same dream of liberty from tyranny that the French had experienced at the hands of their own rulers. No love was lost, either, at that time, between the French and the British. One year after having heard the pivotal news from America, in 1777, Lafayette defied the directives of his superiors and procured a ship with which to set sail for America.

Lafayette offered his voluntary services to the congress of the United States, and was assigned to serve as a major general under George Washington. Over the next two years, the two soldiers became lifelong friends as Lafayette fought with great distinction and unwavering loyalty to Washington, earning Washington's enduring confidence and respect.

In 1779, Lafayette returned to France to convince the French royal court to support the Americans by sending naval and ground units. Lafayette specified that the French troops should serve under Washington. Because of his efforts, many troops sailed to America and fought with the Americans against England. He himself returned in 1780 to continue to fight in Washington's

army. Along with two other French officers, Admiral Rochambeau and Admiral de Grasse, Lafayette joined forces with Washington and brought about the defeat of the British in Yorktown, possibly the most crucial victory of the Revolution, and the one which ultimately led to its end.

1. The primary purpose of the passage is to

    A. illustrate that the French make superior naval officers.

    B. introduce a hero of the American Revolution who was not an American.

    C. give a historical account of the battle of Yorktown and the officers who won it.

    D. tell the story of the life of a wealthy orphan.

    E. show how international cooperation wins wars.

2. The author would likely agree with which of the following statements?

    A. The French and Americans share a common culture.

    B. All free countries should help other countries in their revolutionary wars.

    C. The French fought the American Revolution for the love of adventure.

    D. America and France share an old friendship and a love for common ideals.

    E. The French maintain a superior naval force to the Americans.

3. The author's tone can best be described as

    A. respectful.   B. erudite.   C. neutral.   D. critical.   E. narrow-minded.

Passage 2

The following passage was written by a former slave who became a celebrated abolitionist in the 1850s and 1860s.

I have never approved of the very public manner in which some of our western friends have conducted what they call the "underground railroad," but which I think, by their open declarations, has been made most emphatically the "upperground railroad." I honor those good men and women for their noble daring, and applaud them for willingly subjecting themselves to bloody persecution, by openly avowing their participation in the escape of slaves. I, however, can see very little good resulting from such a course, either to themselves or the slaves escaping; while, upon the other hand, I see and feel assured that those open declarations are a positive evil to the slaves remaining, who are seeking to escape. They do nothing towards enlightening the slave,

whilst they do much towards enlightening the master. They stimulate him to greater watchfulness, and enhance his power to capture his slave.

We owe something to the slaves south of the line as well as to those north of it; and in aiding the latter on their way to freedom, we should be careful to do nothing which would be likely to hinder the former from escaping from slavery. I would keep the merciless slaveholder profoundly ignorant of the means of flight adopted by the slave. I would leave him to imagine himself surrounded by myriads of invisible tormentors, ever ready to snatch from his infernal grasp his trembling prey. Let him be left to feel his way in the dark; let darkness commensurate with his crime hover over him; and let him feel that at every step he takes, in pursuit of the flying bondsman, he is running the frightful risk of having his hot brains dashed out by an invisible agency. Let us render the tyrant no aid; let us not hold the light by which he can trace the footprints of our flying brother.

4. The primary purpose of this passage is to

   A. encourage operators of the Underground Railroad in their work.
   B. praise the courage of Underground Railroad operators.
   C. condemn the tyranny and inhumanity of slavery.
   D. disapprove of the Underground Railroad.
   E. caution Underground Railroad workers to never speak of their work.

5. The author's attitude toward slave owners can best be characterized as

   A. abhorrence.   C. indifference.   E. apathetic.
   B. deference.   D. compassion.

6. The kind of language used in the passage indicates that

   A. the author is very angry and hopes to incite readers to fight against slavery.
   B. the author is an educated man writing for an educated and influential audience.
   C. the author is writing in an intimate style of a letter to a friend.
   D. the author is a former slave who is minimally literate.
   E. the author seeks to reach an audience of refugee slaves.

Passage 3

Thousands of protesting citizens camped in the freezing rain for weeks. The leading candidate was almost poisoned to death under mysterious circumstances. The United States and many other democratic countries applied diplomatic pressure. The Supreme Court of the land came to a decision and its Congress passed a law. It took unremitting forces on all sides, but in the final analysis, it was the determination and passion of the common citizens that drove the tide of change. The corrupt government finally gave in and on December 27, 2004, the people of Ukraine slipped from under Russian control and a free country was born.

On November 21, 2004, as many Ukrainians cast their votes in a national election, they saw hope for breaking their ties with Russia. They voted for Victor Yushchenko, who promised stronger ties with Europe and the rest of the world. But the election did not work in Yushchenko's favor. After his Russian-backed rival, Victor Yanuchovyk, declared himself the winner of the election and president of Ukraine, the Ukrainians didn't buy it. They were certain that their candidate, Victor Yushchenko, had won the election but that the election results had been rigged.

In fact, thousands of Ukrainians were so angry they left their homes that cold winter day and gathered in town squares to protest. They camped in plastic tents on city streets. They listened to speeches and waved the Ukrainian flag and sang the Ukrainian National Anthem. They wore orange, their chosen color of protest, and that blazing color against the frigid white and gray of the Ukrainian wintery background, was the only warmth they found for weeks.

The Ukrainian people had good reason to believe in the dishonesty of the Russian-backed candidate. They had been oppressed by the Soviet Union for many years. Then, when the Soviet Union fell apart in 1989, Ukraine won its independence. But corrupt, Russian-backed politicians still controlled their government and economy.

Victor Yushchenko

On November 27th, the Ukrainian parliament took a vote and said that it did not support the new president. The people grew more hopeful. On December 3rd, the Supreme Court of Ukraine agreed that the election was a fraud and that another election must take place. Meanwhile, Yushchenko had become very ill, and doctors discovered he had been poisoned: enough dioxin had been put into his blood to kill him. His survival astonished health professionals.

On December 26th, 2004, a second election was held. Observers from around the world watched the election closely to prevent fraud. Yushchenko won. That day he told his Ukrainian supporters that, while Ukraine has been independent since 1989, today they are truly free. The protesters packed their tents and headed home, facing a brighter future because of the courageous events of the "Orange Revolution."

7. The passage implies that

   A. voters camping in city squares after a national election might change the election results.
   B. civil revolution is a powerful tool that can lead to anarchy.
   C. normal citizens have the power to change the world if they stand up for themselves.
   D. Ukraine will become an economic powerhouse of Eastern Europe.
   E. candidates can survive even poison assaults if they have the people's support.

8. The organizational pattern used in the passage is

   A. compare/contrast.   C. cause and effect.   E. information/analysis.
   B. problem/solution.   D. order of importance.

9. The author's attitude toward Russia can best be described as

   A. admiration.   B. disdain.   C. resentment.   D. apprehension.   E. caution.

Chapter 2
Sentence Completion

Have you ever caught yourself finishing someone else's sentences? Most people would consider that a rude trait, but the SAT expects you to skillfully finish thoughts and sentences in the **Sentence Completion** sections. This chapter will explain how a sentence's **meaning** and **tone** enable you to both forecast its direction and accurately anticipate how to complete it. You'll learn how to correctly and accurately finish, round off, and sum up other's thoughts, as if you were finishing their sentences for them. Enjoy the activity—but don't practice it on family and friends.

SENTENCE COMPLETION OVERVIEW

Completing an unfinished sentence requires a clear understanding of the sentence's main idea, or what the sentence wants to tell you. In this chapter, you'll read stand-alone sentences with a variety of topics and tones. The sentence topic by itself will not give clues as to how the sentence needs to be finished, but clues will be found in word meanings, sentence tone, and key words. Any information you need to define the correct word will be in the sentences.

As you go through, take your time learning how to respond to sentence completion items. Use a dictionary to help expand your vocabulary by looking up new words. Once you reach the chapter review, however, use no more than one minute to respond to each item.

Some of the test items will have two blanks to be completed; the rest of the items will have only one blank. Each item will have five choices of words or word pairs from which to choose. SAT test questions will have at least one incorrect choice, known as a "red herring," that is *almost but not quite correct*. Generally, your own experiences will enable you to narrow down the five given choices to two, and one of the two will almost certainly be that red herring. Trust your instincts, but keep in mind the skills presented in this section.

Directions

Each of the following sentences has one or two blanks, and each blank signifies that a word is missing. Below each sentence you will find five words or word pairs, lettered A – E. Choose the word or word pair that, when put in place of the blank, **best** fits the meaning of the sentence as a whole.

> **Example:** Popular movies portray heroic astronauts as _____ individuals; they are shown to be as casual of manner and as _____ of speech as cowhands.
>
> A. excitable, raucous   D. energetic, immoderate
>
> B. laconic, deliberate   E. tedious, forcible
>
> C. irritable, sluggish

Which choice contains the pair of words to best fit <u>both</u> blanks?

Read the sentence aloud and say "blank" to fill in the missing words. Just from reading the sentence you will hear its "tone," whether positive or negative. Now look at the pairs of words. Which ones fit the tone? Also, which words fit into the logic of the sentence?

Explanation: The first part of the sentence describes astronauts as "heroic," a positive reference. Look at the choices and decide which has a positive first word.

- Choices, A, C, and E, may be eliminated immediately; all these word pairs have a negative tone.

- Both B and D have first words which have positive meanings.

- Choice B is the only choice of these two that has a second word which logically matches the second part of the sentence. In this part, a comparison is made with astronauts' attitude and speech to that of cowhands. Cowhands are people whose work with animals demands a calm, measured communication style or speech.

The correct answer is B.

Notice in the example above that knowing the meaning or at least the connotations of words in the sentences gives clues to the type of word needed in the blanks. This chapter contains topics which will allow you to build your word meaning skills.

- Context Clues
- Connotations/Denotations
- Word Derivations, Origins, and Analysis
- Resources: Dictionary and Thesaurus Skills

Word Meaning

Word meaning, or understanding the image, object, or idea represented by words on a page, is basic to any reading activity. Take the word "blog," for example. Blog is a new addition to dictionaries and names the action of posting opinions and information in response to other postings on a common Web page. To read the word "blog," or any other new word, and to understand the idea or concept behind it, a reader would have to use reading comprehension skills.

In the following pages, you will read about four different methods used to find word meaning, not in reading passages but in small, single sentences. Still, the methods are similar: **context clues**, **connotations/denotations**, **word derivations**, **origins**, **analysis**, and **dictionary** and **thesaurus** skills.

Context Clues

CSI, *Law and Order*, *Cold Case*, and countless other police dramas put clues front and center, clues that point to the "who, what, when, where and how" of any mystery or crime. Similarly, clues in a reading passage point to the meaning of unknown words and save you from having to consult a dictionary. Your reading will be more effective when you learn how to ferret out word meaning clues by understanding their context.

Context clues refer to the words and ideas surrounding a word. Here, context refers to words which are present in a stand-alone sentence. There are different types of context clues. Some signal a **definition**; some signal a **contrast** in the text. Still others signal **examples**, **comparisons**, or **time.** The table following lists different context clues with explanations and examples.

Context Clues	Signal Words
Comparison	*also, and, both, in addition to, in the same way, like, likewise, resembling, similarly, than, the same as, too*
	Look for clues that indicate an unfamiliar word is similar in meaning to a familiar word or phrase.
	Example: By himself, that young man could **vocalize** just *like* the Mormon Tabernacle Choir and Elvis Presley combined.
Contrast	*although, but, different than, even though, however, in contrast, in spite of, instead of, nevertheless, not, notwithstanding, on the one hand, on the other hand, rather, regardless, still, unlike, whereas, while, yet*
	Look for clues that indicate an unfamiliar word is opposite in meaning to a familiar word or phrase.
	Example: Emma has great **aspirations** to be a Broadway dancer, *yet* right now she is a tremendously talented shortstop.

Context Clues	Signal Words
Definition or Restatement	*in other words, in short, is, meaning, or, that is, "to be" verbs, which* Look for words that define the term or restate it in other words. **Example:** My uncle has never recovered from his love of **sophomoric** humor, *meaning* that he tells puns and plays practical jokes without end.
Example	*after all, even, for example, for instance, in fact, specifically, such as, the following example, to illustrate,* a dash *(—), or* a colon *(:)* Look for examples used in context that reveal the meaning of an unfamiliar word. **Example:** Student drivers need to be taught motoring **nuances**, such as when to use blinkers, how much distance to keep from cars, when *not* to use cell phones, and what is an appropriate moment to change radio stations.
Time	*after, after a few days, afterwards, as long as, as soon as, at last, at that time, before, earlier, immediately, in the meantime, in the past, lately, meanwhile, now, presently, simultaneously, since, so far, soon, then, thereafter, until, when* **Example:** For a few hours, Dewey was thought to be the **victorious** candidate *until* all votes were tallied, revealing Truman as the true victor.

How can you apply context clues in sentence completion test items? A sentence with a single phrase is normally a definition sentence. When signal words alert you to a definition, example, or summary in a sentence, the sentence keeps the same main idea. In a sentence of two phrases, when the signal words alert you to a contrast or time change, one part of the sentence contradicts the other.

Below you will find two sentence completion examples with an explanation of context clues. These explanations will describe how signal words can be used, along with the topic of the sentence, to reveal the correct response.

Example 1: When people _____, they use an Internet application, a Web log, where they can write and post opinions in response to others on a common use Web page.

   A. reboot   B. blog   C. e-log   D. chat   E. surf

Example 2: The revised dress code _____ that all employees must wear the newest uniform; however, after a meeting during which the staff offered concerns, management _____ the directive.

A. suggested, challenged	D. pronounced, ridiculed
B. left out, deleted	E. stipulated, rescinded
C. restated, formalized	

Explanations:

1. In this sentence, you would use **definition clues**, that point either to the definition within the sentence or a restatement (**synonym**) of the missing word. The "to be" verbs such as *are* act as signals alerting you to a definition. The sentence's main idea is that people are using this activity to communicate via the Internet.

   - All the choices are activities used on the Web, except for e-logging (a red herring), but Choices **A**, **C**, **D**, and **E** do not match the explanation.

Choice **B**, *blog*, is the correct response. It is a condensed version of "Web log," the term which is given in explanation.

2. In this example, the clues or key words include a **contrast clue**—*however*. This clue tells you that the missing words are opposites (**antonyms**) of each other. The sentence also tells you about the connection between the two groups: one is employees, the other is management. The main idea is how the two solve a dress code dilemma. Using logic or experiences will help decipher the intent of this sentence.

   - Logic tells you that choices **B**, **C**, and **D** can be eliminated.
   - Choice **B** has two synonyms, but the contrast clue, *however*, proves this incorrect.
   - Choice **C** says management *formalized* the directive, which is not a contrast.
   - Choice **D** offers a contrast in the second word, *ridiculed*, but it is a too extreme word for management.
   - Choice **A** is the "nearly correct" incorrect response, but *challenge* is not logical.

Choice **E** is correct, as the words contrast: the first means *to specify*, the other means *to call back*.

Practice 1:   Context Clues

A. Each of the following sentences has one or two blanks, and each blank signifies a missing word. Below each sentence you will find five words or word pairs, lettered A–E. Choose the word or word pair that, when put in place of the blank, *best* fits the meaning of the sentence as a whole.

1. As the eldest of three brothers, Matthew must utilize all the _____ he can muster to settle sibling arguments.

A. petulance	D. pulchritude
B. sagacity	E. irritability
C. disdain	

2. No matter how much Ana loved reading poetry for pleasure, its _____ gave her some confusion and, occasionally, some low grades.

    A.   gratification   C.   interpretation   E.   artifice

    B.   benevolence   D.   xenophobia

3. The dark, _____ nature of our city park trails prompted not lighting and clearing of the area; rather, it prompted city officials to _____ on personal safety.

    A.   labyrinthine, sermonize   C.   providential, magistrate   E.   sublime, proselytize

    B.   slapdash, editorialize   D.   agoraphobic, serialize

4. To the admiration of all visitors, our local zoo just _____ its orangutan habitat; likewise, visitor conveyances have been _____, so it is possible to go off-road and into the new natural habitat.

    A.   imputed, enhanced   D.   refurbished, modified

    B.   scrutinized, truncated   E.   bolstered, enshrouded

    C.   subsidized, exonerated

B. On a separate sheet of paper, write the context clues and identify the type of each you found in the items, and give an explanation of the correct response.

Practice 2: Create Sentences to Complete with Clues

Write four sentences, two with one blank and two with two blanks. Use a different type of context clue for each. Then create five choices for the blanks, including one correct response. Share your sentences with your instructor, tutor, or peers. Are your reader(s) able to choose the correct answer and tell you why it is correct?

CONNOTATIONS/DENOTATIONS

Although word meanings seem as straightforward as answers to clues, they are sometimes slippery and resist a single definition. Word meanings, especially in the realm of emotional overtones or associations, can change over time. These are called word **connotations**. The dictionary meanings, the **denotations**, change more slowly, lagging behind the changes in popular usage.

For example, the two verbs **pontificate** and **orate** mean virtually the same thing—to lecture on a subject. This is the denotative meaning for both. In the past, these two words had a positive connotation of sharing knowledge with others.

Now however, the word "pontificate" has a negative connotation of being stuffy and self-aggrandizing. The word "orate," on the other hand, has kept a positive connotation.

When completing sentences it is important to be aware of word connotations and denotations alike. Connotations can twist the intent of the sentence from something positive to negative, and vise-versa.

Example: Colonel McClure piloted many flights to exotic lands; he used these adventures as a basis for _____ about procedures to eager recruits.

A. pilfering   C. simulating   E. pontificating

B. orating   D. precipitating

- Choices **A**, **C**, and **D** have nothing to do with public speaking.

- Choice **B**, "orating," would match the positive nature of the rest of the sentence.

- Choice **E** has a negative connotation and does not fit the tone.

So, **B** is the correct response.

Practice 3: Connotations and Denotations

A. Each of the following sentences has one or two blanks, and each blank signifies that a word is missing. Below each sentence you will find five words or word pairs; lettered A–E. Choose the word or word pair that, when put in place of the blank, *best* fits the meaning of the sentence as a whole.

1. But one _____ solution stimulates other problems that must then also be considered as possibilities within the "String Theory" experiment.

    A. hypothetical   D. gregarious

    B. imaginary   E. aromatic

    C. redundant

2. Eleanor Roosevelt had the _____ nerve to voice her opinion and even take civic actions which were _____ by the administration.

    A. unmitigated, unsanctioned   D. tentative, exhumed

    B. unadulterated, reviled   E. careful, suggested

    C. ubiquitous, endorsed

3. Since first gaining audience attention in the 1928 cartoon short "Steamboat Willie," Mickey Mouse has become increasingly childish; his demeanor has _____ from a sly prankster to a warm-hearted innocent, while his body has grown _____ and more rotund.

    A. coalesced, fatter   D. decried, exonerated

    B. increased, stabilized   E. softened, plumper

    C. culminated, atrophied

4. Although political theory has become almost a(n) _____ on talk shows, the essential ideas have become lost in the contentious nature of the "talk" format.

    A. comedy   C. anachronism   E. diversion

    B. exigency   D. superfluous

5. Bee mites can be _____ in domesticated bee hives by consistent utilization of specialized herbs and chemicals; however, feral bee populations cannot be _____ where consistent pest control is impossible.

   A. endemic, prevalent   D. exterminated, salvaged

   B. annihilated, decimated   E. redeemed, established

   C. noxious, recouped

6. Many humorists employ _____ to make a point to a jest; likewise, those whose write in a philosophical tone use _____ to reinforce a message.

   A. quips, sonatas   C. epigrams, parables   E. rhetoric, idioms

   B. sermons, equations   D. acronyms, allegory

B. On a separate sheet of paper, write the connotations (if any) and the denotation for each correct word choice, and give an explanation for why it is the correct response.

Practice 4: Create Sentences to Complete with Connotations and Denotations

Write four sentences, two with one blank and two with two blanks. Use a different type of context clue for each. Then create five choices for each blank, including one correct response. Use as many choices which share a common meaning—but different connotation—as you can. Trade your sentences with peers or share them with your instructor or tutor. Are your reader(s) able to choose the correct answer? Discuss the effect that connotations and denotations have on the item choices.

WORD DERIVATIONS, ORIGINS, AND ANALYSIS

Words have within them clues to their meanings, even in the smallest word units: **prefixes**, **roots**, and **suffixes**. Root words, especially, play a vital role in the vocabulary of the English language. One root word may provide the basis for a multitude of similar words. Many words are derived from one; this is known to language experts as **word derivation**.

Think about the word "vocal." It comes from the Latin root word *vox*, meaning "to call, voice." Some of the words related to "vocal" which derive from the root word *vox* are voice, vocalization, revoke, irrevocable, and vocabulary. In contemporary English most **word origins** come from the Latin, Greek, Norse, and Old Anglo-Saxon languages.

These languages comprise most of the word origins in the English vocabulary. The language of the Anglo-Saxons was Germanic, so English developed as a Germanic language. All major languages, and some "minor" ones, have had an influence on the English language, since it has absorbed vocabulary from practically everywhere. The reasons for borrowing words include the repeated invasions of England, along with trading with other countries for goods that the island could not produce.

Below is a brief chart showing some common words and roots from the earliest Norse, Latin, and Greek influences:

Norse: Norse words comprise roughly 2% of all common English vocabulary. Closely related to the Anglo-Saxon, the two are difficult to separate. Usually Anglo-Saxon and Norse words were simple, and after France invaded England in 1215, they were considered not fit for the upper class to speak.

rót	root, something pigs did when looking for food
leggr	leg
samr	same
skinn	skin; most words which begin with sk- are Norse, such as *sky* and *skill*

Latin:

-gress-	to walk: digress, transgress, progress, congress
-dict-	to say: dictate, predict, edict, contradict
-agri-	fields: agriculture, agriculturalist, agria
-amor-	love: amicable, amorous, enamored, amateur

Greek:

-stat-	to stay: static, stability, iconostasis
-dem-	people: pandemic, democracy, endemic
-path-	feeling: sympathy, apathy, empathy, empathetic, telepathy
-phon-	sound: telephone, phonetics, cacophony, symphony

When we break down words into their smallest units, we **analyze** the words. Take, for example, the word *cosmopolitan*. What does it mean exactly? The prefix, *cosmo-*, is from the Greek word *kosmos*, meaning "universe, order." The root is from the Greek word, *politikon*, meaning "affairs of state." When we combine the small units of *cosmopolitan*, we understand the definition as "having a social world-view or perspective."

Countless other words may be understood in this same way. For example, the simple word *detect* has two parts and comes from the Latin word *detegere*. The root word, *tegere*, means "cover," and the prefix *de-* means "un- or off." So when you put the two parts together, you get "un-cover." That's what you want to do when using word derivations and analysis for completing sentences at the SAT—uncover word meanings.

A section with relevant Web sites with lists of common French, Latin, Greek, and Norse words or root words appears at the end of this chapter. See the following tables for examples of word parts.

PREFIXES

Prefix	Meaning	Example	Prefix	Meaning	Example
ab-	from	absolve	in-	not	involuntary
ad-	to	administer	inter-	between	interrupt
anti-	against	antidote	intra-	within	intramural
com-	with	compunction	post-	after	postdated
de-	reverse, remove	debilitate	pre-	before	premature
dis-	apart, away	disparage	pro-	before, onward	pronounce
en-	in	envisage			
ex-	out	expunge	re-	back, again	recant
il-	not	illusion	sub-	under	subliminal
			un-	not	unbearable

ROOTS

Root	Meaning	Example	Root	Meaning	Example
ann	year	annuity	multi	many	multitude
aqua	water	aquatic	path	feeling	pathological
aud	hear	auditory	phon	sound	phonetic
bio	life	biosphere	port	carry	rapport
cent	hundred	centipede	rad	ray	radiant
chron	time	chronicle	scope	see	telescope
dic	to speak	dictionary	scrib	to write	subscribe
gen	race, kind	generation	tele	distance	telecast
ject	throw	trajectory	ven	to come, go	convention
med	middle	mediator	viv, vit	life	survive, vitality

SUFFIXES

Suffix	Meaning	Examples	Suffix	Meaning	Examples
-able	capable of being	notable, bearable	-ly	in a like manner	eminently, miserly
-age	related to	disparage, salvage	-less	without	doubtless, endless
-al, -ial	act of, of, like	diurnal, primordial	-logy	study of	geology, zoology
-ance	state or quality of	countenance, endurance	-ment	condition of	habiliment, parliament
-er, -or	one who	teacher, editor	-ness	quality, condition	giddiness, worthiness
-ful	full of	regretful, gleeful	-ous	full of	abstemious, egregious
-hood	state of	neighborhood, statehood	-ship	position held	penmanship, township
-ish	having quality of	squeamish, replenish	-tion	action, state of being	defalcation, inhibition
-itis	inflammation	appendicitis, tonsillitis	-ure	process of	censure, indentured
-ive	having the nature of	combative, imputative	-ward	in a specified direction	onward, backward

Below are two sentence completion items with explanations of word derivation and analysis. These explanations describe how word parts and signal words are used, in conjunction with the sentence topic, to reveal the correct response. Read the sentences and decide which choice would be the best response. Then check the explanations.

Example 1: In 1890, a Swedish gentleman sold his body to science as he desperately needed cash; thus, when he had two teeth _____, he had to pay damages for removing body parts without permission.

A. extracted   C. absorbed   E. censured

B. remediated   D. dehydrated

Example 2: On September 8, 1908, as the Chicago Cubs and the New York Giants were tied in a crucial game, one of the Giants _____ thought his team had scored the winning run; as he left the field, he was pronounced "out," _____ the teams to play again.

A. nefariously, wresting

B. posthumously, divulging

C. facetiously, maneuvering

D. erroneously, obliging

E. unctuously, retaliating

Explanations:

Example 1 is fairly straightforward. In the second clause, *thus* shows comparison or explanation that the body parts were removed. What word would be similar to "remove?" Look at the choices for their word parts for clues to a similar word.

- Choice **A** is possible, since the prefix "ex" means *out* and "tract" means *to draw*. But is this the best response?

- Choice **B** has a similar prefix, but the root word means *to settle something*.

- Choice **C**'s prefix means *from* and the root means *to take in*—this is not the same as "removing," which is *moving out*.

- Choice **D** has a prefix, de-, which means *remove*, but the root "hydrate" means *water*.

- Choice **E** has Latin origins; the word means *judgment*.

Choice A, extract or *draw out*, is the best response—it is most similar to "remove."

Example 2 is a story-type item. You will need to follow the time element and use your own experiences to choose the logical word pair. In the sentence's first part, a player "thought" his team had won, but the sentence goes on to contradict that. Analyze the choices to be sure of the correct response.

- Choice **A** has unusual word parts: Latin, "ne-" means *not* ; "fari" means *right, divinely spoken* ; "-ous" means *full of = full of not right*. This seems too strong for what the player did. But checking the second word, "wresting" means *to take by force*—this does not quite fit two baseball teams finishing a game.

- Choice **B** is a more common Latin word: "post" means *after* ; "humous" means *to bury = after death*. This choice cannot be correct.

- Choice **C** is derived from the Latin word "facetia," meaning *a joke*. The player was not being funny— not correct.

- Choice **D** has a root word "error" meaning *wander* or *go astray*—this is fits the logic of the sentence—does the second word also match? Root word "oblige" means to *bind by oath*. Since team sports implies an agreement to conduct a fair contest, the two teams <u>can</u> be said to be *obliged* to play out the game later.

- Choice **E**: "unctuous" comes from the Latin meaning *act of annointing*. Later the word changed to mean *oily* as oil was used to annoint people. Clearly incorrect.

So, choice **D** has the pair of words which fit the logic of the sentence.

Practice 5: Word Derivations, Origins, and Analysis

A. Each of the following sentences has one or two blanks, and each blank signifies a missing word. Below each sentence you will find five words or word pairs; lettered A–E. Choose the word or word pair that, when put in place of the blank, *best* fits the meaning of the sentence as a whole.

1. Antidisestablishmentarianism is a sterling example of a(n) _____ word since it has too many syllables to be taken seriously in conversation.
   - A. perfidious
   - B. agglomerate
   - C. multisyllabic
   - D. abhorrent
   - E. multifarious

2. A confident person must achieve self-direction and organization; _____ behavior will not benefit a successful lifestyle.
   - A. piquant
   - B. ubiquitous
   - C. voracious
   - D. inchoate
   - E. pedantic

3. Although normally a(n) _____ artist, Tintoretto painted *Israelites Gathering Manna in the Wilderness,* which portrays men armed with _____ shotguns that were not invented until centuries later.
   - A. adroit, anachronistic
   - B. bombastic, superficial
   - C. volatile, capricious
   - D. apoptotic, whimsical
   - E. competent, catastrophic

4. While never really abandoning his _____ to a higher position in the University of Peking library, Mao Tse-Tung took up a different _____ : becoming chairman of the Chinese Communist party.
   - A. disenchantment, harbinger
   - B. abscission, conformity
   - C. veneration, panegyric
   - D. aspiration, endeavor
   - E. calamity, succor

5. Ferdinand Demara, the "Great Imposter," regretted being discharged as a navy surgeon during the Korean War, but he could be _____ by the knowledge that his _____ treatments were successful.
   - A. empowered, improvised
   - B. assuaged, therapeutic
   - C. mollified, ignoble
   - D. imperiled, pivotal
   - E. stigmatized, sophisticated

B. On a separate sheet of paper, write out the prefixes, roots, and suffixes with their meanings for each correct word choice.

Practice 6: Create Sentences to Complete with Word Derivations and Analysis

Write six sentences, three with one blank and three with two blanks. Be as creative as you can. Then create five choices for each sentence, including one correct response. For the choices, use words which have several syllables with prefixes and suffixes. Trade your sentences with peers or share them with your instructor or tutor. Can your reader(s) choose the correct answer?

DICTIONARY AND THESAURUS SKILLS

This section is a quick summary of resources you should use when preparing for the SAT Reading Test. A listing of Web sites with both dictionary and thesaurus functions, as well as of popular text resource publishers, appears at the end of this chapter.

Dictionaries will provide you with not only word meanings but also word origins, pronunciations, word schematics, and good usage. Online resources, such as Merriam-Webster Online (www.m-w.com) and www.dictionary.reference.com, will provide you with basic material, but printed texts still offer "within-reach" opportunities to explore possible better options in word choice. Only the information necessary for selecting a given best word choice will be covered on the test (and, by extension, this chapter), so studying pronunciation is optional.

The following is an example of a dictionary entry:

> **mu·sic** \myü-zik\ *n.* **1.** The art of composing sounds in order to produce a continuous and evocative composition through melody, harmony, and rhythm. **2.** Vocal or instrumental sounds having aspects of melody, harmony, or rhythm. **3a.** A musical composition. **b.** The written or printed score for a composition. **c.** Such scores considered as a group: *I left my music in a heap on the bench.* **4.** A musical accompaniment. **5.** An aesthetically pleasing or harmonious sound or combination of sounds: *the sound of waves lapping the shoreline was music to all of us.*

PARTS OF SPEECH

Dictionaries denote each word's part of speech. On online dictionaries, most times the entire part of speech classification is given near the word entry, as a heading that separates its various uses. In published texts, the part of speech is usually abbreviated immediately between the word and its given meanings. An abbreviation chart usable with both online and print dictionaries follows below:

adjective = *adj.*	conjunction = *conj.*	noun = *n.*	transitive verb = *vt.*
adverb = *adv.*	interjection = *interj.*	preposition = *prep.*	verb = *vb.*
article = *article.*	intransitive verb = *vi.*	pronoun = *pron.*	

Example: He loudly rehearsed the political speech.

He *pron.* / loudly *adv.* / rehearsed *vb.* / the *article.* / political *adj.* / speech *n.*

DEFINITIONS

Each entry in a dictionary will provide the word meaning, but sometimes there are several definitions given for a single word. For example, the word **needle** has two entries, each with multiple meanings:

1 nee·dle *n.* **1a** a small, slender steel instrument that has an eye for thread at one end and is used for sewing; **b** any of several devices for carrying thread and making stitches . . .

2 needle *v.* tease or goad;

ETYMOLOGY

The **etymology** (word origin) of each word is often included in a dictionary entry. Online dictionaries usually spell out the etymology information, and it may be in a side box, or at the beginning or end. In text dictionaries, the origins are often put into abbreviated form and are typically placed at the beginning of the entry after the part of speech. Some examples of these abbreviations are **OE**, Old English; **Fr**, French; **L**, Latin; **GR**, Greek.

SYNONYMS/ANTONYMS

Synonyms are similar in meaning to the entry word, and **antonyms** are opposite in meaning to the entry word. When included in dictionaries, they are often placed at the end of entries, both in text and online.

THESAURUS

A thesaurus is a word-meaning resource that focuses on the synonyms and antonyms for words. Like a dictionary, it may be found online or in text form.

The following is an example of an online thesaurus entry:

---

fight (n)

altercation, argument; clash, dispute, row, run-in, wrangle, conflict; brawl, clash, combat, hostility, scrap, skirmish, **contest**; bout, competition, match, round

Antonym: reconciliation, retreat, withdrawal

Practice 7:   Dictionary and Thesaurus Skills

Take a few minutes and go through each of the practices in this chapter, looking for unfamiliar words. List any words for which you are unsure of the meaning. Use a dictionary to find the meanings and parts of speech. List the synonyms and at least one antonym for each word. Trade your list with peers or share them with your instructor or tutor.

TONE

The best definition of **tone** is the simplest: style or manner of speaking or writing, including word choices, expressive of a mood or emotion. Normally, in a discussion of tone, there would be numerous types of tones to investigate: happy, angry, bemused, concerned, optimistic, and pessimistic, to name just a few. For now, only two tones will be discussed: **positive** and **negative**.

Tone is a clue which points towards the correct response for many sentence completion items. Some of the items will have a neutral tone. When positive or negative tone is present, however, there may be signal words of comparison, example, or definition to help you complete a sentence.

Be aware that a sentence may be positive in one part and negative in the other, if the parts are separated by a contrast signal word or time signal word.

See the sentence completion examples and explanations below:

Example 1: Nathan plays video games with his usual _____ attention to _____.

A. diligent, detail
B. sacrificial, purification
C. iconoclastic, preference
D. prosaic, vigor
E. judicious, dissonance

Example 2: Bart played video games with his habitual _____ attitude and _____ demeanor.

A. complacent, insouciant
B. intransigent, cordial
C. compliant, malleable
D. combative, surly
E. mellifluous, misogynistic

Example 3: Even though the impact of playing video games may _____ mental quickness, it may be _____ to overall health, depending on the amount of time spent and the time of day played.

A. mitigate, noisome
B. enhance, detrimental
C. obfuscate, supercilious
D. augment, providential
E. impugn, minatory

For Example 1, look at the main words—this person is said to play video games with his *usual attention*—those words are positive in tone. In the five choices, look at the first words—if any are negative, eliminate those choices. When you find a choice with a positive first word, you will want to check that the second word has a positive tone also.

- Choices **B–D** in this example are negative in tone; eliminate those.
- Choices **A** and **E** have positive first words. For Choice **A**, the adjective, *diligent*, means "painstaking" and the word *detail*, means the "fine points." Both words are positive in tone.
- For Choice **E**, the second word, dissonance, means a lack of agreement. It is negative.

So, choice **A** is the correct response.

For Example 2, look again at the wording which appears in the sentence. The person here plays with some sort of *habitual attitude* and *demeanor*. Those words have a negative tone, mostly due to connotations.

- Choices **A**, **C**, and **E** have positive first words, so you can eliminate them.
- Choice **B** has a negative first word but positive second word.
- Choice **D** has two negative words: *combative* means "eager to fight" and *surly* means "churlish."

So, **D** is the correct tonal response.

For Example 3, look carefully at the wording which appears in the sentence, especially any signal words. A contrast signal word (*although*) appears. In the choices, you will want to find contrasting tones, one positive and one negative.

- Choices **C**–**E** have two words with similar tones; eliminate those.
- Choice **A** has a positive word for the first blank, but "mitigate," meaning *to ease* used with "mental quickness" creates a negative idea. "Noisome" is also negative.
- Choice **B** has appropriate positive and negative words.

So, **B** is the correct response.

Practice 8: Tone

Each of the following sentences has one or two blanks, and each blank signifies that a word is missing. Below each sentence, you will find five words or word pairs, lettered A–E. Choose the word or word pair that, when put in place of the blank, <u>best</u> fits the meaning of the sentence as a whole.

1. Kato Mateu's revolutionary _____ hard/soft boot technology pioneered the shoe-style skate design; it acts both as a shoe and a boot with comfort and stability.
   A. lucid   B. insular   C. hybrid   D. viable   E. specious

2. Cornwallis never fooled the Revolutionary army at Green Spring Farm with his _____ military tactics; his battle strategy was plainly _____ with victory.
   A. inept, incompatible   D. haughty, preceded
   B. ponderous, substantiated   E. sated, fraught
   C. submissive, precipitated

3. It will be almost impossible to completely _____ the idea that dolphins are no longer merely intelligent organisms but that they have _____ to intelligent tool-users before our eyes, utilizing sponges as protection for their snouts.
   A. misconstrue, altered   C. dispel, conformed   E. reject, evolved
   B. appreciate, succumbed   D. vindicate, occluded

4. Art murals depicting dogs in space suits _____ the Washington metro L'Enfant Plaza Station, stirring _____ commentary from commuters.
   A. discredit, empathetic   C. grace, defamatory   E. impede, propitious
   B. adorn, amused   D. demean, jovial

5. While endangered snow leopards are still _____, sightings on Mount Everest are a testament to these animals' _____ and offer hope in the foreseeable future.
   A. demagogues, procrastination   D. diurnal, flexibility
   B. unencumbered, convergence   E. surviving, vulnerability
   C. threatened, resilience

Practice 9: Create Sentences to Complete with Tone

Write four sentences, two with one blank and two with two blanks. Then create five choices for each sentence, including one correct response. Use words with negative or positive tones. (Hint: Look at the chart of prefixes for negative word ideas.) Trade your sentences with peers or share them with your instructor or tutor.

STUDENT RESOURCES: WEB SITES AND BOOKS

<u>Web sites</u>

Word Derivations and Origins

Word Quests for Word Seekers
http://www.wordquests.info/

This online dictionary of English word origins specializes in Latin and Greek derivations and includes definitions. Word searches are easy and comprehensive.

Word Wizard
http://www.wordwizard.com/

A site "for lovers of the English language" that offers etymology, a word choice search engine, and plenty of helpful links. Its message board system can make information retrieval tricky but worth the surfing time to explore its abundance of connections.

English words of NORSE origin
http://odin.bio.miami.edu/norse/words.html

The site has a list of familiar English words and their original Old English or Norse form. There is also a link to a thorough history of the English language.

GuruNet, Answers.com: loanwords
http://www.answers.com/topic/loanword

This site has valuable information about "loanwords" —words that English has borrowed from other cultures. There are also numerous links to other sources.

Dictionaries/Thesauruses

OneLook

http://www.onelook.com/

The site has a collection of dictionaries rolled into one, including a dictionary devoted to the etymology of words. Many of the dictionaries linked to the site also have links to thesaurus materials.

Merriam-Webster Online
http://www.m-w.com

The 800-pound gorilla of learning resources offers dictionary and thesaurus search engines on its Web site. Links to premium paid services, such as Unabridged and Collegiate Reference editions, are unobtrusive to the free services on the main page. Free word-of-the-day and games sections add to the bookmarkability.

Dictionary.com
http://www.dictionary.reference.com

This one's name says it all—type a word in its engine, and this site gives you all possible meanings and even some etymology (word history) thrown in for good measure. Look closely for the small tabs beneath the engine blank that allow you to toggle between dictionary, thesaurus, and encyclopedia functions.

Books

Hall, Katherine L. *Reading Stories for Comprehension Success: Senior High Level, Reading Levels 10-12*. San Francisco: JosseyBass, 2004
A workbook with more than 45 factual stories with related teaching materials, packed with story lessons and activities for building your reading, comprehension, and writing skills.

Pintozzi, Frank, and Devin Pintozzi. *Basics Made Easy: Reading Review*. Woodstock: American Book Company, 2000.
If you need to review reading basics before preparing for the SAT, try this easy-to-understand book that condenses basic reading comprehension strategies into an engaging format. This book can help you hone your skills in word meaning, reading comprehension, literature analysis, graphic aids, dictionary skills, and reference sources. Each chapter contains concise lessons and frequent practice exercises, plus ends with an open-ended chapter review followed by a multiple-choice test in a standardized test format.

Random House Webster's Build Your Power Vocabulary. New York: Random House, 1997
A strong vocabulary is a key component to doing well on the SAT Reading Test. This concise vocabulary-building guide has chapters on word roots and affixes, the history of interesting words, and up-to-date vocabulary. It contains sections on spelling and on the differences between American and British English. It also contains a glossary of usage to ensure that you choose the right words and put them in their proper place. Plus, numerous vocabulary tests and exercises, as well as a section of entertaining word puzzles, helps you use your new knowledge.

CHAPTER 2 REVIEW

Each of the following sentences has one or two blanks, and each blank signifies that a word is missing. Below each sentence you will find five words or word pairs: lettered A–E. Choose the word or word pair that, when put in place of the blank, *best* fits the meaning of the sentence as a whole.

1. Because his family had only one computer and took turns using it, Gilbert had to adopt a _____ attitude to complete his semester project.

   A. querulous   C. credulous   E. perseverant

   B. terse   D. predatory

2. Hurricanes are prolonged storm systems from which it is possible for people to be _____, whereas tornados are unpredictable, short-lived events during which people can only stay put in low-lying or permanent structures for protection.

   A. inoculated   C. propitiated   E. levitated

   B. vaccinated   D. evacuated

3. The _____ game of the series only made us that much more anxious to see the season finale.

   A. venerable   C. philanthropic   E. penultimate

   B. intrepid   D. voluminous

4. Since Florence Nightingale first revolutionized nursing, the field has been considered a woman's _____; until about the past two decades, most male nurses have faced some _____ for their profession.

   A. domain, derision   C. burden, pinioning   E. vocation, remorse

   B. resolve, accolades D. calling, endorsement

5. Kudzu is reviled for its _____ growth; it enshrouds every living thing in its path in a strangling veil of dust-green foliage.

   A. propitious   C. splenetic   E. impudent

   B. voracious   D. lugubrious

6. In the humanist philosophy of John Locke, knowledge is _____, not _____; that is, people are reasonable through examining the world around them.

   A. acquired, innate   C. illusory, meretricious   E. transient, ephemeral

   B. conviction, heresy   D. protracted, superfluous

7. The myriad challenges and outright dangers of hiking the Appalachian Trail, demands a hiker be both _____ and _____.

   A. fortuitous, exasperated   C. pretentious, innovative   E. resilient, tactful

   B. vigilant, resilient   D. reclusive, prudent

8. Solar winds, made up of electrically charged ions, periodically meet the earth's _____ yet _____ magnetic field, where ionic particles are caught and spun through the atmosphere as the Northern Lights.

   A. tenuous, frugal   C. tenacious, fluctuating   E. spontaneous, impulsive

   B. erudite, superficial   D. deleterious, tangential

9. Despite its famous name, to assume that the Hanging Gardens of Babylon are actually hanging would be a(n)_____ gaffe; they were actually created by embedding gardens on terraces or balconies.

   A.   exemplary   C.   ostentatious   E.   extenuating

   B.   florid   (D.)   outright

10. The late Secretariat still receives _____ as the racehorse of the ages; no horse before or since has run as fast or shown more "will to win."

   A.   longevity   C.   tirades   (E.)   respect

   B.   lassitude   D.   prosperity

11. Historically, coffee has been an incredibly stimulating beverage; Voltaire drank the _____ amount of 50 cups a day while writing; similarly, Honoré de Balzac kept up an even more _____ level of coffee consumption as he worked.

   A.   extravagant, miserly   C.   amicable, spurious   E.   diligent, abbreviated

   (B.)   prodigious, copious   D.   rosaic, transient

12. What had previously been a watershed victory for the law firm became a(n) _____ public relations disaster, lasting for seven long years.

   A.   hedonist   (C.)   exhausting   E.   ephemeral

   B.   aesthetic   D.   intuitive

13. The 1968 song "MacArthur Park" was conceived by its writer as a _____ myth of lost love; nevertheless, it has been _____ for the humor of its unconventional symbolic lyrics.

   A.   Arthurian, digitized   C.   superficial, abbreviated   E.   pusillanimous, preempted

   (B.)   serious, parodied   D.   aesthetic, enhanced

14. Because the boys were twins and always active, the family expected that they would have similar _____ such as fly fishing, camping, archery, rock climbing, and hang gliding.

   (A.)   vexations   C.   diversions   E.   divestitures

   B.   collaborations   D.   reconciliations

15. I denounce the practice of _____; this is the moment to settle down and become inured in one local culture.

   A.   peregrination   C.   tautology   E.   reconciliation

   (B.)   intransigence   D.   verisimilitude

16. Although the character is supposedly a(n) _____ clown, the actor hardly _____ a classic spirit of sublime merriment.

   A.   saturnine, precipitates   C.   reverent, scrutinizes   (E.)   surreptitious, provokes

   B.   impetuous, recreates   D.   quintessential, evinces

Chapter 3
Critical Reading

Why is the reading section on the SAT labeled **Critical Reading**? "Critical" involves **active** or **thoughtful** reading. To read critically means reading with your mind engaged in questioning and seeking out connections throughout the reading. This active reading functions to broaden and strengthen your understanding of the reading material.

What is the format of the SAT Critical Reading section?

The section will have both short and long passages ranging from 100 to 800 words. Many passages will have an **introduction** in italics. When an introduction is present, be sure to read it as carefully as the passage. It will have explanatory elements important for choosing the correct responses.

The **shorter passages,** usually one paragraph in length, will have two questions; when short passages are paired together, there will be four questions. **Long passages** will have around eight questions each; when long passages are paired, there will be about thirteen questions. Some questions for paired passages focus on each passage individually, but some will ask you to compare or contrast relationships between the two passages. The SAT reading passages have an assortment of topics and disciplines, such as humanities, literary fiction, social studies, and sciences. They also have varied styles of writings, such as persuasive, narrative, and expository.

You will utilize similar skills to engage in active reading and to answer questions for both the short and long passages. However, there are different strategies for managing the different passage lengths.

Consider each of these critical skills as stations in a routine, like stations on an obstacle course. The best tactic for developing targeted skills is to read often and according to the stipulations of each particular station. The more you practice, the better prepared you will be for the SAT.

Skills

1st Station: Main Ideas

2nd Station: Details/Vocabulary in Context

3rd Station: Inferences/Conclusions

4th Station: Compare/Contrast Paired Passages

Strategies: Scanning/Skimming

1ST STATION: REACH FOR MAIN IDEAS

When reading a passage, you will want to read for the **main idea**—the essential or basic message. Every author has a basic idea to communicate, and it is a reader's task to recognize that idea. The passage's main idea may be directly stated by the author or it may be implied.

The strategies for identifying a main idea fluctuate to some extent with the length of the passage.

DIRECTLY STATED MAIN IDEA — SHORT PASSAGE:

In a short passage of a single paragraph, the main idea is typically established in the title, opening sentence, or final sentence. Pay particular attention to these elements when you read a short passage. Determine what you consider the main idea to be; then scrutinize each of the choices and select the one closest to your solution. As an example:

Marian Anderson

In a dramatic and celebrated act of conscience, Eleanor Roosevelt resigned from the Daughters of the American Revolution (DAR) when it barred the world-renowned singer Marian Anderson, an African American, from performing at its Constitution Hall in Washington, DC. Following this well-publicized controversy, the federal government invited Anderson to sing at a public recital on the steps of the Lincoln Memorial. On Easter Sunday, April 9, 1939, some 75,000 people came to hear the free recital. The incident put both the artist and the issue of racial discrimination in the national spotlight...

Excerpted from the National Archives website, *www.archives.gov*

The main idea of this passage is that

A. performing at Constitution Hall was an ordeal for people who disagreed with the values of the Daughters of the American Revolution (DAR).

B. Marian Anderson was a popular singer in the 1930s, except in the Washington, DC, area and its environs.

C. the free show on Easter Sunday, April 9, 1939, was sponsored by the federal government and was well attended by about 75,000 people.

D. there were many social issues in the 1930s, including discrimination against women, which needed attention.

E. Marian Anderson being barred but later invited to perform in Washington, DC, brought national awareness to racial discrimination.

Explanation:

Did you form the answer for yourself before reading the choices? Remember, that is one way you may avoid "almost-right" choices that the SAT is known for.

- Choices **A** and **C** are ideas found in the passage which support the main idea.

- Choices **B** and **D** are not completely true according to the information in the article: the performance at the Lincoln Memorial speaks to Marian Anderson's popularity, and the passage does not directly address gender discrimination.

Choice **E** paraphrases the last sentence, which directly gives the main idea of the passage. The "incident" includes the resignation of Eleanor Roosevelt, the barring of Marian Anderson, and the subsequent invitation extended to her by the federal government in recognition of DAR's discrimination.

DIRECTLY STATED MAIN IDEA — LONG PASSAGE

For a passage of several paragraphs, it would be to your advantage to **skim**, or quickly read, the passage, but the particular type of skimming essential in the SAT is a modified form. It is modified because, while you will want to read through the material quickly to seek out the more important elements, you will want to carefully note the passage title and the opening and final sentences for each paragraph. It is through evaluating the information in these elements that you will identify the directly stated main idea. Also take note of significant or repeated words in the passage. Read quickly but with focus, and determine what you think the main idea is before reading the choices. Practice this strategy with the following passage:

Government Guidelines on Equal Pay

When the Equal Pay Act was first proposed there was much acrimonious debate over what constitutes equal work. Historically, men and women had clearly delineated roles in a work place. In the Industrial Age, those categories became blurred as men and women began to work side by side on assembly lines. While in such close quarters, wages could not be kept private. Women knew they were receiving less pay for their work on the line. After some time and false starts, the government was able to achieve a definition of equal pay satisfying most everyone.

The Equal Pay Act requires that men and women be given equal pay for equal work in the same establishment. The jobs need not be identical, but they must be substantially equal. It is job content, not job titles, that determines whether jobs are substantially equal. Specifically, the EPA provides that employers may not pay unequal wages to men and women who do equal work, or perform jobs that require substantially equal skill, effort, and responsibility, and that are performed under similar working conditions within the same establishment.

Job skills are measured by factors like the experience, ability, education, and training required to perform the job. The key issue is what skills the job requires, not what skills the individual employees may have. For example, two accounting jobs could be equal under the EPA even if one of the employees has a master's degree in physics, since that degree would not be required.

Effort in a position is defined as the amount of physical or mental exertion needed to perform the job. For example, suppose that men and women work side by side on a line assembling machine parts. The person at the end of the line must also lift the assembled product as he or she completes the work and place it on a board. That job requires more effort than the other assembly line jobs . . . As a result, it would be correct to pay that person more, regardless of gender.

The concept of responsibility is shown by the degree of accountability required in the job. For example, a salesperson who is delegated the duty of determining whether to accept customers' personal checks has more responsibility than other salespeople. On the other hand, a minor step in responsibility, such as turning out the lights at the 5:00, would not justify a pay differential.

Pay differentials are permitted when they are based on seniority, merit, quantity or quality of production, or a factor other than [gender]. These are known as "affirmative defenses" and it is the employer's burden to prove that they apply.

Adapted from Government EEOC Web site

Which of the following best states the main idea of the passage?

A.   Skill level determines if men and women receive equal pay for the position.

B.   Equal pay for men and women depends on the responsibility levels required for the position

C.   Equal pay for men and women depends on the effort levels, physical and mental required for the position.

D.   The Equal Pay Act requires that men and women be given equal pay for equal work in the same establishment.

E.   Employers do not have to follow the equal employment opportunity guidelines when they can show that males are better suited for work by citing "affirmative defenses."

Explanation:

It is imperative for a long passage that you form a response about the main idea independently and prior to reading the choices. There is a substantial amount of material which can distract you from the essential elements in determining the main idea.

- Choices **A–C** are ideas developed within the passage which support the main idea.

- Choice **E** is not absolutely factual (males are not attributed with superior ability) according to the passage. Be suspicious of choices similar to Choice E. This type of choice utilizes specialized vocabulary (in this case, "affirmative defenses") embedded in the passage but often misuses it or makes the choice too specific to be the main idea.

Choice **D** is the main idea supported by the other ideas, alluded to, or hinted at in the title and directly stated at the beginning of the first paragraph.

Tips for Finding a Stated Main Idea
1. **Read the title.** The main topic of the paragraph or passage is often mentioned in the title.
2. **Read the entire paragraph or passage.** You'll get an overview of who or what the selection is about.
3. **Read the first and last sentence of each paragraph.** Most of the key words and ideas will be stated in these places.
4. **Choose the answer that is the best statement or restatement of the paragraph or passage.** Your choice should contain the key words mentioned in the title, the first sentences, or the last sentences of each paragraph or passage.

IMPLIED MAIN IDEA — SHORT PASSAGES:

It is critical for this section and the one subsequent that you understand exactly what is meant by an **implied main idea**—to imply something means to furnish clues or hints for an idea or message. The pursuit of an implied main idea requires the reader to pursue different strategies. The passage will offer facts and details which allude to or hint at a main idea, but it will not state a main idea directly in a tidy, single sentence. This is the occasion to read between words and between the lines and to determine what the author did not say and what the author did say. What was considered worthwhile to include to get a message to readers, and in what tone was it framed?

The **tone,** positive, negative, or neutral will also contribute to your understanding of the main idea. Determining tone means asking *how* the author uses words in the passage; are the words positive, negative, or neutral? This is critical to know when you have narrowed the choice of responses down to two, and one is positive while the other is negative.

For the short passage, read meticulously for **key words,** which are repeated in some form throughout the paragraph. Additionally, listen for the tone of the paragraph. Through these strategies, determine what you believe the main idea to be. Then scrutinize the choices, and select the one which most closely resembles your own response. Practice this procedure with the next example.

The symphony of the present age has perhaps fallen somewhat in estate. It was natural that it should rush to a high perfection in the halcyon days of its growth. It is easy to make mournful predictions of decadence. The truth is the symphony is a great form of art, like a temple or a tragedy. Like them it has had, it will have its special eras of great expression. Like them it will stay as a mode of utterance for new communities and epochs with varying nationality, or better still, with vanishing nationalism.

Symphonies and Their Meaning; Third Series, Modern Symphonies, by Philip H. Goepp

The main idea for this passage is that

A. symphonies rise and fall in popularity and in excellence through the ages.

B. at the time the passage was written, the symphony was lost as an art.

C. during early halcyon days, the symphony seemed permanently ordained as a high calling.

D. the symphony is a great, high form of art endlessly giving style and voice to new cultures.

E. predicting the symphony's ascent into decadence is premature in this time.

Explanation:

- Choices **B** and **C** are ideas embedded in the passage which support the main idea.

- Choice **D** is what the article says is not absolutely accurate.

- Choice **E** is close to being true—but has a vocabulary error— "decline," not ascent, would be accurate. Furthermore, the tone of that selection is a predominantly negative one, too negative to correspond with the passage's intent.

Choice **A** synthesizes the supporting ideas, pulling them together in a positive manner, to compose the implied main idea. Choice **A** is the correct response.

IMPLIED MAIN IDEA — LONG PASSAGES:

For long passages, follow the same directions for directly stated main ideas, but now read between the lines. Since the main idea is implied, seek clues and hints as to the main idea in the paragraphs. You will still want to utilize the modified skimming technique for key or repeated words in the passage. Read quickly but with focus, and identify the main idea before reading the choices. Practice this strategy with the following passage:

Excerpt from *The Folklore of Plants*, by T. F. Thiselton-Dyer

The author of this passage has written numerous books about folklore. In this passage, the connections between beliefs in witchcraft and the belief in the curative powers of plants are blended.

[An] anecdote current in Yorkshire is interesting, showing how fully superstitions of this kind are believed: "A woman was lately in my shop, and in pulling out her purse brought out also a piece of stick a few inches long. I asked her why she carried that in her pocket. 'Oh,' she replied, 'I must not lose that, or I shall be done for.' 'Why so? I inquired. 'Well,' she answered, 'I carry that to keep off the witches; while I have that about me, they cannot hurt me.' On my adding that there were no witches nowadays, she instantly replied,

'Oh, yes! There are thirteen at this very time in the town, but so long as I have my rowan-tree safe in my pocket they cannot hurt me.'"

Occasionally, when the dairymaid churned for a long time without making butter, she would stir the cream with a twig of mountain ash, and beat the cow with another, thus breaking the witch's spell. But to prevent accidents of this kind, it has long been customary in the northern countries to make the churn-staff of ash. For the same reason herd-boys employ an ash-twig for driving cattle, and one may often see a mountain-ash growing near a house… No tree, perhaps, holds such a prominent place in witchcraft-lore as the mountain-ash, its mystic power having rarely failed to render fruitless the evil influence of these enemies of mankind.

… The herb-bennett (Geum urbanum), like the clover, from its trefoiled leaf, renders witches powerless, and the hazel has similar virtues. Among some of the plants considered antagonistic to sorcery on the Continent may be mentioned the water-lily, which is gathered in the Rhine district with a certain formula. In Tuscany, the lavender counteracts the evil eye, and a German antidote against the hurtful effects of any malicious influence was an ointment made of the leaves of the marsh-mallow. In Italy, an olive branch which has been blessed keeps the witch from the dwelling, and in some parts of the Continent the plum-tree is used.

What main idea is the author trying to convey?

A. The mountain ash is renowned for its protection against witches.
B. All plants are believed to keep people safe from Harry Potter's sorcery.
C. Many plants have healing properties that will heal the ill-effects of witches.
D. A belief in the supernatural led people to develop natural protections against evil spirits.
E. Knowing the names and power of each plant in the local area is what kept people safe from the malicious influences around them.

Explanation:

- Choices **A–C** are ideas found in the passage which support the main idea.
- Choice **E** is not completely true according to the passage; though it uses specialized vocabulary, "malicious influences."

Choice **D** is the main idea supported by the other ideas; it is hinted at in the introduction and directly stated at the beginning of the first paragraph. Choice **D** is the correct response.

Tips for Determining an Implied Main Idea

1. **Read the title.** The title will help you identify the topic of the selection.

2. **Read the entire paragraph or passage.** You will get a general understanding of the selection.

3. **Re-read the facts and details in each paragraph.** Think of overall ideas they share in common.

4. **Choose the answer that summarizes all of the facts and ideas in the passage.** Confirm your choice by going back to the passage to check your evidence one more time.

Practice 1: Main Ideas — Stated and Implied

Read each passage below and respond to the questions which follow based on its content (stated or implied) and on any introductory material.

Excerpt from *Dream Psychology: Psychoanalysis for Beginners* by Sigmund Freud

In what we may term "prescientific days" people were in no uncertainty about the interpretation of dreams. When they were recalled after awakening they were regarded as either the friendly or hostile manifestation of some higher powers, demoniacal and Divine. With the rise of scientific thought the whole of this expressive mythology was transferred to psychology; today there is but a small minority among educated persons who doubt that the dream is the dreamer's own psychical act.

1. Is the main idea stated or implied? ~~Stated~~ implied

2. What main idea is the author trying to convey?
    A. Dreams have no real reason for occurring as they do.
    B. Most intelligent people know that dreams are psychological in origin.
    C. Dreams used to be considered the product of other worldly influences.
    D. Educated people doubt that dreams are the dreamer's psychical act.
    E. Dreams mythology has kept people from recalling them clearly.

Excerpt from *Two Thousand Miles on an Automobile* by Arthur Jerome Eddy

This whole question of paying for services in connection with automobiling is as interesting as it is new... [the] automobile… is still sufficiently a curiosity to command respect and attention. The farmer is glad to have it stop in front of his door or put up in his shed; he will supply it with oil and water. The blacksmith would rather have it stop at his shop for repair than at his rival's—it gives him a little notoriety, something to talk about. So it is with the

liveryman at night; he is, as a rule, only too glad to have the novelty under his roof, and takes pride in showing it to the visiting townsfolk. They do not know what to charge, and therefore charge nothing. It is often with difficulty anything can be forced upon them; they are quite averse to accepting gratuities; meanwhile, the farmer, whose horse and cart have taken up far less room and caused far less trouble, pays the fixed charge.

3. Is the main idea stated or implied? __implied__

4. The main idea of this passage is that
    A. When automobiles toured towns, they were charged less than horse and cart.
    B. In their early years, automobiles used to draw paying crowds when drivers took the cars touring in the countryside.
    C. Different professions would argue over who got to display visiting cars.
    D. Farmers who kept driving horses and carts paid more for overnight stays than cars.
    E. Anything new, like the automobile, takes precedence over the old, like horse and cart, it is replacing.

Excerpt from *Manners and Social Usages*
by Mrs. John M. E. W. Sherwood

Nothing strikes the foreigner so much (since the days of De Tocqueville, the first to mention it) as the prominent position of woman in the best society of America. She has almost no position in the political world. She is not a leader, an intrigante in politics, as she is in France. We have no Madame de Stael, no Princess Belgioso, here to make and unmake our Presidents; but women do all the social work, which in Europe is done not only by women, but by young bachelors and old ones, statesmen, princes, ambassadors, and attaches. Officials are connected with every court whose business it is to visit, write and answer invitations, leave cards, call, and perform all the multifarious duties of the social world.

5. Is the main idea stated or implied? __stated__

6. Which of the following best states the main idea of the passage?
    A. Women direct the social duties of America, which surprises other countries where men, too, take an active role in managing these aspects of society.
    B. Women in America have always been social equals to men in the official ambassador duties.
    C. Women are not political leaders in America though many European countries have female royalty in power. These women are called by De Tocqueville the "intrigante."
    D. Women, globally, have the prominent position of controlling the multifarious duties and manners of the social world.
    E. Women have in the recent past made and unmade presidents through their inherent social powers.

Excerpt from *A General History and Collection of Voyages and Travels, Vol. VIII.*
by Robert Kerr (1755–1813)

Refreshing ourselves one day here, we went forwards three days more, with our camels, and came to Aleppo, where we arrived on the 21st of May. This has the greatest trade, for an inland town, of any in all those parts, being resorted to by Jews, Tartars,

Persians, Armenians, Egyptians, Indians, and many different kinds of Christians, all of whom enjoy liberty of conscience, and bring here many different kinds of merchandise. In the middle of the city there is a goodly castle, raised on high, having a garrison of four or five hundred janissaries. Within four miles round about there are many goodly gardens and vineyards, with many trees, which bear excellent fruit, near the side of the river, which is very small. The walls of the city are about three miles in circuit, but the suburbs are nearly as large as the city, the whole being very populous.

7.   Is the main idea stated or implied?_____

8.   What main idea is the author trying to convey?

   A.   This city of Aleppo has a rural aspect in the farms, an urban center with the castle, and suburbs outside of the city walls.

   B.   Aleppo must be a city off the normal trade routes as it took a long trip on camels to arrive there.

   C.   Aleppo, an inland city, is an impressive, bustling multicultural site, attracting free trade and thought.

   D.   The city of Aleppo was visited by Jews, Tartars, Persians, Armenians, Egyptians, Indians, and many different kinds of Christians, all there to trade.

   E.   With so much trade activity in the town of Aleppo, a large garrison of soldiers is required to keep the peace,

The Taste of the Present Age [1876]

The material in this passage refers to another age. The authors see disturbing trends in 1800s England, and are voicing their concerns in plain language.

Amongst many other distinguishing marks of a stupid age, a bad crop of men, I have been told that the taste in writing was never so false as at present. If it is really so, it may perhaps be owing to a prodigious swarm of insipid trashy writers: amongst whom there are some who pretend to dictate to the public as critics, though they hardly ever fail to be mistaken. But their dogmatic impudence, and something like a scientific air of talking the most palpable nonsense, imposes upon great numbers of people, who really possess a considerable share of natural Taste; of which at the same time they are so little conscious as to suffer themselves passively to be misled by those blundering guides.

But the Taste in writing is not, cannot be worse, than it is in music, as well as in all theatrical entertainments. In architecture indeed there are some elegant and magnificent works arising, at a very proper time to restore the nation to some credit with its neighbors in this article; after its having been exposed to such repeated disgraces by a triumvirate of awkward clumsy piles, that are not ashamed to show their stupid heads in the neighborhood of Whitehall: and one more, that ought to be demolished; if it was for no other reason but to restore the view of an elegant church, which has now for many years been buried alive behind the Mansion-house.

It is indeed some comfort, that while Taste and Genius happen to be very false and impotent in most of the fine arts, they are not so in all. The arts of Gardening particularly, and the elegant plan of a farm, have of late years displayed themselves in a few spots to greater advantage in England, than perhaps ever before in any part of Europe. This is indeed very far from being universal; and some gardens, admired and celebrated still, are so smoothly regular, so over-planted, and so crowded with affected, impertinent, ridiculous ornaments of temples, ruins, pyramids, obelisks, statues, and a thousand other contemptible whims, that a continuation of the same ground in its rude natural state, is infinitely more delightful. . . .

Excerpt from *Essays on Taste*, by John Gilbert Cooper, John Armstrong, Ralph Cohen

9. Is the main idea stated or implied?_____

10. What is the author's main idea in this passage?

   A.   Gardens, to be considered Art, should be left as natural as surrounding vacant fields.

   B.   While Taste and Genius happen to be very false and impotent in most of the fine arts, they are not so in all.

   C.   Questionable Taste in writing has corrupted other fine arts and their patrons.

   D.   The Genius of Architecture is gaining ground after some regrettable missteps by the previous triumvirate of "bad men."

   E.   Natural good Taste is being nullified by artificial Taste which was introduced by critical, self-satisfied writers.

2ND STATION: DETAIL/ VOCABULARY IN CONTEXT

Any system of support requires balance: wheels support the weight of a car, table legs support tables, and your health is supported by balanced nutrition. **Details**, including specific **vocabulary words**, are all about balance. As you read through a passage, you will discover countless details which the author incorporates into the text, supporting the main idea.

The SAT passages are are teeming with details supporting the main ideas. Details answer questions about the passages such as *who, what, when, where, why,* and *how:* the standard 5 Ws and H. The strategies for retrieving detail information vary with the length of the passage. The questions are often formatted with a **not** or **except**, as in, "All the choices below are correct except . . ." In this format, you must read each of the choices carefully and quickly identify which of the choices are present in the passage and which one is not.

DETAILS — SHORT PASSAGES

For a short passage of one paragraph, details are fairly simple to retain in memory. When responding to short passages, you may want to read the questions **first**; the SAT limits the questions at two for each short passage. When you read the questions first, you will recognize exactly which details to remember. The same is true for the questions which will ask you to choose the context meaning of certain words. The vocabulary questions will ask what a certain word means in the sentence. So, you will watch for how the word fits into the meaning of the paragraph as a whole. Practice these two test items with the next example.

In a dramatic and celebrated act of conscience, Eleanor Roosevelt resigned   **1**
from the Daughters of the American Revolution (DAR) when it barred the
world-renowned singer Marian Anderson, an African American, from
performing at its Constitution Hall in Washington, DC. Following this
well-publicized controversy, the federal government invited Anderson to sing at   **5**
a public recital on the steps of the Lincoln Memorial. On Easter Sunday, April
9, 1939, some 75,000 people came to hear the free recital. The incident put both
the artist and the issue of racial discrimination in the national spotlight. . .

Excerpted from the National Archives website: *www.archives.gov*

1. In line 4, the incident is described as well-publicized because

    A. it occurred in 1938, when the radio had become common in households.

    B. the free recital was given at the Lincoln Memorial on Easter Sunday for about 75,000 people visiting Washington, DC.

    C. it was the first resignation by Eleanor Roosevelt's daughter in the American Revolution.

    D. a dramatic act of conscience was committed on behalf of Marian Anderson, a world-renown singer.

    E. the federal government stepped in to make the controversy worse and thrust it into the national spotlight.

2. The term "issue" in line 8 most closely means

    A. emergence.   B. offspring.   C. outlet.   D. problem.   E. publication.

Explanations:

For **question 1**, choice **D** is the correct response as it describes the two elements of the incident: Marian Anderson's world wide status and the noted act of conscience by Eleanor Roosevelt. While choice **A** is not found in the text, choices **B** and **E** describe events after the incident (E does so incorrectly), and choice **C** confuses the information.

For **question 2**, all the options are synonyms of the word "issue." In the context of Eleanor Roosevelt's resignation from the DAR and the free public recital for Marian Anderson the best choice for the meaning would be problem (**D**), as in a national problem of racial discrimination.

DETAILS — LONG PASSAGES

In a long passage of up to 800 words, details can be obscured by the amount of text. Fortunately, the SAT formatters number the lines by 5s. When a detail or vocabulary question is asked, it will pinpoint the lines you need to read to find the specific details. You will want to read a few lines before and after the section to have a clear understanding of the material's context. Practice this process with the following example, which you read earlier for main idea:

Excerpt from *The Folklore of Plants*
by T. F. Thiselton-Dyer

The author of this passage has written numerous books on folklore. In this passage, the connections between beliefs in witchcraft and the belief in the curative powers of plants are blended.

[An] anecdote current in Yorkshire is interesting, showing how fully superstitions of this kind are believed: "A woman was lately in my shop, and in pulling out her purse brought out also a piece of stick a few inches long. I asked her why she carried that in her pocket. 'Oh,' she replied, 'I must not lose that, or I shall be done for.' 'Why so?' I inquired. 'Well,' she answered, 'I carry that to keep off the witches; . . .There are thirteen at this very time in the town, but so long as I have my rowan-tree safe in my pocket they cannot hurt me.'" **5**

Occasionally when the dairymaid churned for a long time without making butter, she would stir the cream with a twig of mountain ash, and beat the cow with another, thus breaking the witch's spell. But, to prevent accidents of this kind, it has long been customary in the northern countries to make the churn-staff of ash… No tree, perhaps, holds such a prominent place in witchcraft-lore as the mountain-ash, its mystic power having rarely failed to render fruitless the evil influence of these enemies… **10 15**

… The herb-bennett (Geum urbanum), like the clover, from its trefoiled leaf, renders witches powerless, and the hazel has similar virtues. Among some of the plants considered antagonistic to sorcery on the Continent may be mentioned the water-lily, which is gathered in the Rhine district with a certain formula. In Tuscany, the lavender counteracts the evil eye, and a German antidote against the hurtful effects of any malicious influence was an ointment made of the leaves of the marsh-mallow. In Italy, an olive branch which has been blessed keeps the witch from the dwelling, and in some parts of the Continent the plum-tree is used. **20 25**

1. In the first two paragraphs of the passage (lines 1–18), the author suggests that witchcraft could interfere with humans
   A. when the special herbs or plants were forgotten or misapplied by accident.
   B. when milkmaids did not churn the butter correctly.
   C. when there were at least thirteen witches in the area.
   D. when mountain ash trees are not given room to grow.
   E. as the superstitions about the evil eye were not believed by everyone in the vicinity.

2. In line 1, "current" most nearly means
    A. flow.   B. recent.   C. money.   D. movement.   E. running.

Explanations:

For **question 1**, choice **A** is the correct response, as in the first story the woman fretted about losing her "rowan stick" and butter is not churned because of an accidental hexing—and so the cow had to be beaten. Choice **B** is a result not a cause, choices **C–E** are not suggested as causes.

For **question 2**, all the options are synonyms of the word "current." In the context of an anecdote (story) in a certain region (Yorkshire), choice **B** is the correct response. The other choices have the meaning of the word as movement of water or wind in tides or direction of flow and one meaning as it applies to money.

Practice 2: Details/Vocabulary in Context

Read each passage below and respond to the questions which follow based on its content (stated or implied) and on any introductory material.

It is difficult to determine exactly when First Lady Mary Todd Lincoln   **1**
(1818–1882) lost confidence in George McClellan. The Union general's
reluctance to capitalize on the advantage he had gained over Confederate forces
in the Battle of Antietam just two months earlier had guaranteed his removal as
commander of the Army . . . if Mary Todd Lincoln disliked McClellan for his   **5**
lack of aggression, she despised Gen. Ulysses S. Grant for exactly the opposite
reason. Thus her apparent change of heart toward McClellan may have been as
much political as military wisdom. Both men had such a large following,
McClellan with Peace Democrats and Grant with Republicans of every stripe,
that they threatened her husband's grip on the presidency.   **10**

From the Library of Congress: *American Memory*

1. In line 3 "capitalize" most nearly means

    A. to write or print with a beginning capital or in capitals
    B. to gain by turning something to an advantage
    C. to compute present value of
    D. to convert into capital funds
    E. to use as a seat of government

2. Which of the following was **not** a reason for Mary Todd Lincoln's loss of confidence in George McClellan?

    A. the loss at the Battle of Antietam
    B. his lack of aggression
    C. his close friendship with General Grant
    D. his reluctance to turn an advantage for the Union army
    E. a large following and popularity with Democrats

The British Connection

Every nation, like every individual, is born free. Absolute freedom is the birthright of every people. The only limitations are those which a people may place over themselves. The British connection is invaluable as long as it is a defense against any worse connection sought to be imposed by violence. But it is only a means to an end, not a mandate of Providence of Nature. The alliance of neighbors, born of suffering for each other's sake, for ends that purify those that suffer, is necessarily a more natural and more enduring bond than one that has resulted from pure greed on the one side and weakness on the other. Where such a natural and enduring alliance has been accomplished among Asiatic peoples and not only between the respective governments, it may truly be felt to be more valuable than the British connection itself, after that connection has denied freedom or equality, and even justice.

1

5

10

Excerpt from *Freedom's Battle*, by Mahatma Gandhi

3. In line 9 "bond" most nearly means
    A. permanent glue.
    B. legal attachment.
    C. link in a chain.
    D. uniting influence.
    E. monetary guarantee.

4. In lines 6 and 7, saying "not a mandate of Providence of Nature" Gandhi suggests that
    A. taking cues from the natural world, India should violently overthrow the British.
    B. despite a limit on freedoms, India should always keep a close connection to Britain.
    C. the connection to Britain is the means to an end, or a satisfactory government profile, for India.
    D. as a colonial protectorate of Britain, India should make the best of the restricting situation.
    E. the rule of Britain is impermanent and an unnatural arrangement.

Excerpt from *The Folklore of Plants*, by T. F. Thiselton-Dyer

An immense deal of legendary lore has clustered round the so-called fairy-rings—little circles of a brighter green in old pastures—within which the fairies were supposed to dance by night. This curious phenomenon, however, is owing to the outspread propagation of a particular mushroom, the fairy-ringed fungus, by which the ground is manured for a richer following vegetation. Amongst the many other conjectures as to the cause of these verdant circles, some have ascribed them to lightning, and others have maintained that they are produced by ants.

1

5

These fairy-rings have long been held in superstitious awe; and when in olden times May-dew was gathered by young ladies to improve their complexion, they carefully avoided even touching the grass within them, for fear of displeasing these little beings, and so losing their personal charms. At the present day, too, the peasant asserts that no sheep nor cattle will browse on the mystic patches, a natural instinct warning them of their peculiar nature. A few miles from Alnwick was a fairy-ring, round which if people ran more than nine times, some evil was supposed to befall them.

10

15

5. In the first paragraph, the author suggests that the legendary lore of fairy-rings
   A. extends to the livestock which browse inside the circles of grass.
   B. is not completely true but manufactured to keep strange people out of the fields.
   C. has not had much impact on the populace despite the propagation of it.
   D. is easily explained by natural phenomena—mushrooms, ants, or lightning.
   E. may be blamed on the fact that the supernatural creatures danced only at night.

6. In line 3 "curious" most nearly means
   A. odd.   B. unmatched.   C. obtrusive.   D. prying.   E. inquisitive.

3RD STATION: INFERENCES AND CONCLUSIONS

If it takes strong focus to identify main ideas and good balance to identify details, then identifying **inferences** and **conclusions** takes flexibility. You will need to flex your mind around ideas which are not directly stated in a passage and think beyond the passage, flexing your insight beyond the text, to reach a conclusion.

For inferences and conclusions, all the information needed to respond to test items will be in the passages. For the inferences you will need to use the same process as when you looked for implied main ideas—reading between the lines of the text. What did the author not say, and what did the author say?

> **Example:** During the game, umbrellas bloomed in rainbow colors throughout the stadium as players wiped mud from their eyes with long sleeves.

What inference could you make about the weather during the game?

Of course, it is raining and perhaps cold since the uniforms are long-sleeved. You know this from the text and your own experience with inclement weather. For conclusions, you will use the material in the text and your knowledge and experience.

Read the questions *first* for the short passages, so you will know what to look for when reading the passage itself. For long passages, you will want to read them and note any inferences or conclusions as you go. Practice the two types of flexing—between lines (inferences) and outside the box (conclusions) by reading the following passage, answering the questions, and looking at the explanations.

La Salle's Voyage to the Mouth of the Mississippi (1682)
by Francis Parkman

The Indians of this village were the Natchez; and their chief was brother of the great chief, or Sun, of the whole nation. His town was several leagues distant, near the site of the city of Natchez; and thither the French repaired to visit him. They saw what they had already seen among the Taensas—a religious and political despotism, a privileged caste descended from the sun, a temple, and a sacred fire. La Salle planted a large cross, with the arms of France attached, in the midst of the town; while the inhabitants looked on with a satisfaction which they would hardly have displayed, had they understood the meaning of the act...

1

5

10

1. It can be inferred that "inhabitants looked on with a satisfaction" (line 8) because they

    A. thought the wood could be used for their sacrifice to their sun god.
    B. expected special treatment and to be shown official rites and elaborate ceremony.
    C. appreciated carving and woodworking art in any form.
    D. thought that La Salle was going to make them place the cross and were then relieved when he took the task upon himself.
    E. wanted to put a statue in the middle of town, but this imported cross was even better

2. The second part of the last line, "while the inhabitants looked on with a satisfaction which they would hardly have displayed, had they understood the meaning of the act. . . ." is evidence that

    A. the Natchez people lacked knowledge of French religious rites.
    B. by this act of planting a cross, the French had found a way to ingratiate themselves with the Natchez people.
    C. the French meant to invade the neighboring tribes with the aid of the Natchez.
    D. La Salle was claiming the land belonging to the Natchez in the name of the French king.
    E. the cross was marking the place where La Salle planned to build a church for the Natchez people.

Explanations:

For **question 1**: Did you read the question first? If you did, you would be looking for reasons why these people would feel "satisfied" at this event. To answer an inference question, you will need to note specific words used and details included in the passage. Here, the inference will have something to do with how the Natchez people viewed themselves. The passage begins with a description of how their leader was well regarded, how they had an elite caste system, and how La Salle came to see them. Choice **B** is the correct response based on information in the passage and on basic human nature. Choices **A** and **C** suppose information not given in the passage—the cross may not have been wood. Choices **D** and **E** also suppose information not in the passage—La Salle himself may not have planted the cross and statues may not have been part of their culture.

For **question 2**: Again, reading the question first would focus your attention on the situation. The correct response is choice **D**. Planting the cross with the "arms of France," which would not be welcomed by the Natchez, brings us to the conclusion that France will be colonizing or claiming this part of North America. La Salle and his fellow travelers had been studying the Natchez society and were ready to take some type of action. The other choices lack evidence: no other mention is made of religion, no evidence is given for attacking other tribes, and there are no clues that the French wanted to ingratiate themselves.

Practice 3: Inferences/Conclusions

Read each of the following passages and choose the response which best answers the questions based on the passages' content (stated or implied).

Excerpt from *Henry the Second*, by J. R. Green

King of England, Duke of Normandy, Count of Anjou, Maine, and Touraine, Count of Poitou, Duke of Aquitaine, suzerain lord of Britanny, Henry found himself at twenty-one ruler of dominions such as no king before him had ever dreamed of uniting… His subjects told with pride how "his empire reached from the Arctic Ocean to the Pyrenees;" there was no monarch save the Emperor himself who ruled over such vast domains. But even the Emperor did not gather under his sway a grouping of peoples so strangely divided in race, in tongue, in aims, in history. No common tie of custom or sympathy united the unwieldy bundle of states bound together in a common subjection; … to all England was "another world"—strange in speech, in law, and in custom. And to all the subjects of his heterogeneous empire Henry himself was a mere foreigner.

1. In lines 1 and 2, the passage describes the unique assembly of citizens under Henry's rule, suggesting that

   A. his empire will be invaded by another ruler or rulers.
   B. he will be replaced by the emperor due to an uprising of citizens due to different nationalities, languages, and cultures.
   C. as a suzerain lord, Henry will be compelled to pledge allegiance to one country, benefiting that one but losing control of all others.
   D. Henry will be given title of Emperor, replacing the one who held power before his kingship.
   E. despite a difficult beginning, Henry the Second will grow into his role as an empire builder.

The First Child of European Race Born in America

One summer a ship came from Norway to Greenland. The skipper's name was Thorfinn Karlsefni … who was a very wealthy man, passed the winter there in Greenland, with Lief Ericsson. He soon set his heart upon a maiden called Gudrid, and sought her hand in marriage.

That same winter a new discussion arose concerning a Vineland voyage. The people urged Karlsefni to make the bold venture, so he determined to undertake the voyage, and gathered a company of sixty men and five women...

They sailed to sea with the ship, and arrived safe at Lief's booths, and carried their hammocks ashore there. They were soon provided with an abundant supply of food, for a whale of good size and quality was driven ashore, and they secured it. Their cattle were turned out on the land. Karlsefni ordered trees to be felled; for he needed timber to load his ships. They gathered some of all the products of the land: grapes, all kinds of game, fish, and other good things.

In the summer after the first winter the Skrellings [natives] were discovered. A great throng of men came forth from the woods; the cattle were close by and the bull began to bellow and roar with a great noise. At this the Skrellings were frightened and ran away with their packs, wherein were gray furs, sables, and all kinds of skins… The Skrellings put down their packs, then opened them and offered their wares in exchange for weapons, but Karlsefni forbade his men to sell their weapons...

Now it is to be told that Karlsefni caused a strong wooden palisade to be constructed and set up around the house. It was at this time that a baby boy was born to Gudrid and Karlsefni, and he was called Snorri. In the early part of the second winter the Skrellings came to them again in greater numbers than before, and brought with them the same kind of wares to exchange… The Skrellings seemed contented at first, but soon after, while Gudrid was sitting in the doorway beside the cradle of her infant son, Snorri, she heard a great crash made by one of the Skrellings who had tried to seize a man's weapons. One of Karlsefni's followers killed him for it.

"Now we must needs take counsel together," said Karlsefni, "for I believe they will visit us a third time in greater numbers. Let us now adopt this plan: when the tribe approaches from the forest, ten of our number shall go out upon the cape in front of our houses and show themselves there, while the remainder of our company shall go into the woods back of our houses and hew a clearing for our cattle. Then we will take our bull and let him go in advance of us to meet the enemy." The next time the Skrellings came they found Karlsefni's men ready and fled helter-skelter into the woods. Karlsefni and his party remained there throughout the winter, but in the spring Karlsefni announced that he did not intend to remain there longer, for he wished to return with his wife and son to Greenland. They now made ready for the voyage and carried away with them much in vines and grapes and skins.

Excerpt from "Saga" by Hauk Erlendsson

2. In lines 36–37, Karlsefni's reactions to the Skrellings' attempted theft of weapons suggest that
    A.   he has encountered situations such as these before.
    B.   the Skrellings have the upper hand, and he knows it.
    C.   he wishes he had not tried to settle here.
    D.   the safety of the women and children is his chief concern.
    E.   his primary concern is with the livestock, without which the explorers would starve.

3. The first two paragraphs describing the structure and provisions of the group suggest that
    A.   the group could establish a permanent colony on the North American continent.
    B.   as shelter was available, the success of the venture could be assured.
    C.   with the balance of men to women being uneven, there could be no colony.
    D.   the provisions will not keep the travelers healthy enough to sustain a colony.
    E.   the voyage was fruitful as whales were scarce in Greenland.

4. The last four lines are evidence that
    A.   the Skrellings will continue to chase the invaders by boat.
    B.   Karlsefni will never return but will stay in Greenland with his family.
    C.   the agricultural boon in this new land will draw Karlsefni back.
    D.   Karlsefni will return with other explorers.
    E.   Lief Erickson will make the trek after seeing what Karlsefni has brought back.

4TH STATION: COMPARISONS/CONTRASTS OF PAIRED PASSAGES

Paired passages present a perfect opportunity for comparing and contrasting. In the SAT Critical Reading section, both short and long passages may be paired. The passage **comparisons** are similar to parallel bars (a horizontal path)—they function as guides pointing out similarities between passages. The passage **contrasts**, on the other hand, are like uneven bars (for turning upside down)—they function as guides pointing out the differences in passages—even a 180-degree turn in perspective.

Note: The line numbers for the paired passages run consecutively. The two passages will be presented first and the set of questions after.

Follow the process for answering **short passage** questions: First, read the questions for the first passage, and then read that passage and respond. Next, read the questions for the second passage, and then read the second passage and respond to the questions. Finally, read the questions pairing the passages, and then skim over both passages and respond to questions.

For **long passages**, you will want to read the first passage, marking it up with notes about the main idea, key words, or repeated phrases and then answer the questions which ask only about that one passage. Next, read the second passage, marking it up and responding to its questions. Then read the questions for both passages and skim the passages if you need to refresh your memory about the text.

ANNOTATION STRATEGIES

Since it is important that you keep the ideas of both long passages in mind, it is imperative that you use the opportunity to mark in the SAT test booklet, **annotating** (explaining to yourself) key ideas and details. The following passage is annotated as an example of annotation strategies:

Star Power

How do we describe the elusive, magnetic, and mystical quality known as charisma? <u>People with the gift of charisma are said to be natural leaders or natural stars; people have followed these leaders into war, into peace, and into a shared perspective of what can be.</u> Some of these leaders have been Patrick Henry, Mahatma Gandhi, Adolph Hitler, John F. Kennedy, Margaret Thatcher, Martin Luther King, and Bill Clinton. Some of these stars have been Marilyn Monroe, John Wayne, Lena Horne, Sidney Poitier, Mel Gibson, and Will Smith. What have they had in common? Some researchers have attempted to articulate or measure charisma. They have found <u>six characteristics</u> which give a person potential for charisma: <u>emotionally expressive, enthusiastic, eloquent, visionary, self-confident and responsive to others.</u> Even with these six qualities, however, a person may be simply interesting, not arresting. Researchers are divided on the question of whether charisma is part of a person's DNA or if it is nurtured in life-experiences.

main idea is that charisma is a gift and is natural

details of charisma

In other words, is charisma a <u>purely inherent gift</u> or can training turn a person with no charisma potential into an inspiring leader, or even into a star? Most researchers say no training can bestow such a multi-faceted ability on an individual, mainly because the response of an audience to a charismatic leader is likened to a mystical awarenes—it is <u>immediate and automatic</u>.

tone almost lighthearted, positive charisma is gift

casual relationship?

Given just one quick look of about thirty seconds or so and people can judge if someone else has the <u>emotional intelligence, grace of expression, and the physical attractiveness</u> of a naturally charismatic individual. The combination of traits seems to be the key. A charismatic person must have the verbal and physical confidence and expression to bring an audience to be in sync with them and then to use a sense of timing to <u>amplify</u> that effect until the audience is virtually locked into the message of the leader or into the performance of the star. <u>The political and entertainment "star" image is apt—one that is a natural phenomena of intense brightness and powerful gravitational pull from a distance.</u>

details of charisma and key combination

use of metaphor or imagery for main idea

Practice the process with the following two short passages—read, respond, and check out the explanations:

Passage 1

Natural history specimens were once an essential part of all general   **1**
museum collections. Indeed, many museums were founded on them as
manifestations of the Victorian desire to classify and apply systematic
nomenclature to the natural world. Until relatively recent times, for most
visitors, the museum experience meant rooms filled with minutely labeled   **5**
animals and birds, and sometimes a diorama or group depicting a particular
habitat or a dramatic scene from nature, suitably red in tooth and claw.
Specimens, often in the form of game trophies, were a commonplace in country
houses too. Now, changing attitudes and legislation have demoted natural
history collections from their former prominence in main display areas to the   **10**
oblivion of long-term storage, disposal or even destruction…. Present unease
about the origins of natural history specimens is understandable….

Excerpt from *Conservation of Natural History Specimens* by Robert Entwistle, et al

Passage 2

Congratulations, you caught your first fish.
The brightly-hued blue-gill measures about a foot
and weighs almost two pounds Thrilled and
impatient for others to witness this triumph, you   **15**
imagine transporting it home. Consider this option
carefully: consider a lake odor in the car and the ick factor when your
fascination wanes. Alternatives do exist: have your fish professionally mounted
for display. For this, photograph the fish from multiple angles, and after   **20**
releasing the fish into the lake, take the pictures to a local taxidermy shop.
Taxidermists nowadays mostly mount fish from photographs, utilizing wood
resins and polymers instead of the mummified body for display. Your replica
will be painted matching the original exactly. The procedure began as a
conservation tactic to preserve fish populations. The satisfaction you experience   **25**
in contributing to the balance of nature will outweigh even your substantial
trophy.

1. The main idea of both passages is that

A. attitudes towards hunting animals and catching fish for the dinner table have changed.

B. people do not collect and donate live animals the way they have done in the past.

C. natural history museums and taxidermist shop owners have had to learn new marketing and public relation skills to stay relevant.

D. concern for natural populations has changed the way in which people collect animal specimens or trophies.

E. changing preferences for art and visual displays have caused an upheaval in museums and in country homes.

2. In passage 1, line 7, the phrase "red in tooth and claw," suggests that

    A. the unease mentioned at the passage's end may be due to the actual violent end which these animals suffered.

    B. natural history museums try to heighten the effect or illusion of danger to draw crowds away from the antiquated mounted specimens display.

    C. taxidermists in the museums are using too much red paint to simulate bloody battles.

    D. these are prey animals—hunted by other animals, usually in cooperative packs.

    E. people use the various mounted specimens as teaching devices, warning young children to stay away from wild animals.

3. Passage 2, line 18 describes what happens when a live fish is taken home, suggesting that

    A. the person will need to clean the car seats.

    B. the fish will not live long after the person loses interest.

    C. blue gills are common fish and should not be mounted.

    D. coolers are sufficient containers for live fish.

    E. people need to cook the fish as soon as they get home, so it will be fresh.

4. The authors of both passages would agree that a "conservation tactic" (Passage 2, line 25) means to

    A. mandate a cultural change by non-outdoors people.

    B. keep the wild things in the wild, instead of stuffing them for display.

    C. force people to better plan what they hunt and fish for, leaving indigenous animals alone.

    D. put fish back in lakes for others to catch if they are too small to keep.

    E. take photographs of any animals you harvest before having them mounted.

Explanations:

If you read the specific questions for each passage, you will know what to look for in the passage itself.

Question 1 refers to both passages. The last two sentences of each passage give the main ideas. Choice **D** is the correct response: both passages are concerned with the changes in harvesting animal displays. Choice **A** mentions the dinner table but neither passage considers eating the animals; choices **B** and **E** mention details about donating animal displays and visual displays in country homes which are not part of Passage 2

Question 2 is specific to passage 1. The phrase "red in tooth and claw," is a cliché describing dangers in the natural world which animals face. Choice **A** is the correct response. Choices **B**, **C**, and **E** do not have evidence to support them. Choice **D** mislabels the animals— those with bloodied teeth and claws would be animals of prey.

Question 3 is specific to passage 2. This is an inference question—if you read the lines carefully, they mention "fascination waning" meaning that choice **B** is correct. Choices **A**, **C**, and **D** do not have the evidence or clues in the passage to support them. Choice **E** implies that the fish is to be eaten which is not indicated by any other clue in the passage.

Question 4 also refers to both passages. Choice **B** is the correct response as both passages are concerned with the changing ideas of collecting animal specimens or trophies. The other choices either are not part of both passages or there are no clues to support them.

Practice 4: Compare/Contrast Paired Passages

Read each of the following passages. Questions follow the passages—choose the response which best answers the questions based on the passages' content (stated or implied) and on any introductory elements. Paired passages may also have questions which explore the relationship between the paired passages.

Passage 1

Excerpt from *Human Nature in Politics, Third Edition*
by Graham Wallas

A party tune is equally automatic in its action, and, in the case of people with a musical "ear," even more effective than a party color as an object of emotion. As long as the "Marseillaise," which is now the national tune of France, was the party tune of the revolution its influence was enormous. Even now, outside of France, it is a very valuable party asset. It was a wise suggestion which an experienced political organizer made in the Westminster Gazette at the time of Gladstone's death, that part of the money collected in his honor should be spent in paying for the composition of the best possible marching tune, which should be identified for all time with the Liberal Party. One of the few mistakes made by the very able men who organized Mr. Chamberlain's Tariff Reform Campaign was their failure to secure even a tolerably good tune.

1

5

10

Passage 2

The US national anthem has been under fire intermittently, beloved then hated, since first proposed. Most everyone knows "The Star Spangled Banner" was written by Francis Scott Key while gazing from a window in Baltimore Harbor during heavy shelling by the British—and seeing the US flag flying despite adversity. Actual bombs were "bursting in air," and it is this line that bursts throats and ear drums as average humans attempt to sing it "on Key." But the history still rings true; the original inception of the tune as part of baseball games occurred as it was sung in a ballpark during the World Series of 1917, honoring troops fighting in WWI. The emotional rendering was reenacted in every game thereafter, entrenching the tune in American hearts. Then, on March 3, 1931, Congress designated the song as the US national anthem, 116 years after Francis Scott Key set pen, or quill, to parchment.

15

20

25

Francis Scott Key

1. Both passages support which of the following conclusions about the efficacy of national anthems?

    A. Anthems are best kept for entertainment purposes.
    B. The music composed to match words is rarely, if ever, harmonious.
    C. Anthems stir emotional reactions of patriotic fever from citizens matched by no other.
    D. Whether marching tunes or grinding dirges, anthems are taken too seriously for popular taste.
    E. The uneven marketing of anthems comes from free distribution as political propaganda.

2. In passage 1, line 11 "secure" most nearly means
    A. trustworthy.   C. dependable.   E. provide.
    B. assured.   D. safe.

3. In passage 2, lines 19–21 describe what it is like to sing the anthem, suggesting that
    A. the lyrics are not clear to most people and should be displayed wherever sung.
    B. the music is repetitive and can become a chore to sing over and over.
    C. the melody sweeps the people along until emotion brings tears to every eye.
    D. some notes in the song are difficult for normal people and only professionals should sing it.
    E. a new national anthem should be chosen—a more popular song is "America the Beautiful."

4. Which of the following best describes the main ideas of both passages?
    A. The main idea of passage 1 is that the French national anthem is appropriate in words and music, but the main idea of passage 2 raises concerns of the effectiveness of the US anthem.
    B. Emotional attachments to national anthems defy logic and musical ability.
    C. The main idea in passage 1 raises the idea of political motivations behind national anthems while the main idea of passage 2 strongly refutes this.
    D. Citizens respond more to "party colors," also known as flags, than music.
    E. Passage 1 would give choice of national anthems to political party leaders, but passage 2 would give the choice to average citizens.

CHAPTER 3 REVIEW

Read each of the following passages. Choose the response which best answers the questions based on the passages' content (stated or implied) and on any introductory elements. Paired passages may also have questions which explore the relationship between the paired passages.

These paired paragraphs are about human character. They are both written from philosophical viewpoints.

Passage 1:

Excerpt from *The Life of Reason* by George Santayana

The Greek, too, would not find in our world the things he valued most, **1**
things to which he surrendered himself, perhaps, with a more constant
self-sacrifice — piety, country, friendship, and beauty; and he might add that his
ideals were rational and he could attain them, while ours are extravagant and
have been missed. Yet even if we acknowledged his greater good fortune, it **5**
would be impossible for us to go back and become like him. To make the
attempt would show no sense of reality and little sense of humor. We must dress
in our own clothes, if we do not wish to substitute a masquerade for practical
existence… The movement of conscience has veered; the center of gravity lies
in another part of the character. **10**

Passage 2:

Excerpt from *Human Nature In Politics, Third Edition* by Graham Wallas

Mr. G. K. Chesterton some years ago quoted from a magazine article on
American elections a sentence which said: "A little sound common-sense often
goes further with an audience of American working men than much high-flown
argument. A speaker who, as he brought forward his points, hammered nails
into a board, won hundreds of votes for his side at the last Presidential election." **15**
The "sound common-sense" consisted, not, as Mr. Chesterton pretended to
believe, in the presentation of hammering as logical argument, but in an orator's
knowledge of the way which force is given to non-logical inference and a
willingness to use that knowledge.

1. Which of the following best describes the difference between passages 1 and 2?

    A. Passage 1 uses a change of values from ancient Greece to present day to question where we are headed, while passage 2 describes a speech and its fallacies, questioning modern values.

    B. Passage 1 notes that oratory force, if applied correctly, will change hearts, while passage 2 describes a basic change in the make up of character in modern Americans.

    C. Passage 1 is written with wry humor and imagery of people masquerading in false values, while passage 2 voices appreciation for author Chesterton for pretending the speech was honest.

    D. Passage 1 creates a negative tone regretting the loss of values like piety, country, friendship, and beauty, while passage 2 is positive, portraying political activism as all for the good.

    E. Passage 1 offers a solution which is to be true to whatever values we have embraced, while passage 2 just presents a short event and leaves the reader to agree or disagree.

2. In line 12, "sound" most nearly means
    A. voice.   B. severe.   C. solid.   D. noise.   E. thorough.

3. In line 14, the speaker hammering nails into a board suggests that
    A. the points he was making were being blunted like nails in wood.
    B. he thought his audience needed visual aids to understand the political speech.
    C. he imagined that wooden boards are like some opinions—hard to get through.
    D. the impression he has of his audience is that they needed to hear sound for "sound common-sense."
    E. he wants to convey the message that he could build on the strong points he was making.

4. Unlike the author of passage 1, the author of passage 2 develops a point by relying on
    A. historical context.   C. direct quotation.   E. quantifying materials.
    B. firsthand experience.   D. scientific hypothesis.

**Excerpt from *Henry the Second*
by J. R. Green**

  In the war of Toulouse in 1159, the problem was for the first time raised as **1**
to the obligation of feudal vassals to foreign service, and Henry gladly seized
the opportunity to carry out his plan yet more fully. The chief vassals who were
unwilling to join the army were allowed to pay a fixed tax or "*scutage*" instead
of giving their personal service. Henry, the chroniclers tell us, careful of his **5**
people's prosperity, was anxious not to annoy the knights throughout the
country, nor the men of the rising towns, nor the body of yeomen, by dragging
them to foreign war against their will; at the same time he himself profited
greatly by the change. The new system broke up the old feudal array, and set the
king at the head of something like a standing army paid by the taxes of the **10**
barons.

5. In line 9, "array" most nearly means
    A. adorn.   B. finery.   C. marshal.   D. militia.   E. attire.

6. The last two lines of the passage describing the new look of the army suggest that

    A. King Henry will continue to appease his knights through land grants and indulgences.

    B. with this well-funded army, Henry will be successful in military decisions.

    C. the war of Toulouse will last for many more decades.

    D. most barons will soon tire of paying for pointless, bloody wars.

    E. the fixed tax will be raised for each year the war of Toulouse lasts.

The next two paired passages refer to plants as natural medicines in different eras and disciplines.

Passage 1:

Excerpt from Chapter XXI, *Plants in Folk-Medicine* by T. F. Thiselton-Dyer

From the earliest times plants have been most extensively used in the cure of disease, although in days of old it was not so much their inherent medicinal properties which brought them into repute as their supposed magical virtues. Oftentimes, in truth, the only merit of a plant lay in the charm formula attached to it, the utterance of which ensured relief to the patient. Originally there can be no doubt that such verbal forms were prayers, "since dwindled into mystic sentences."… **5**

…Of the thousand and one plants used in popular folk-medicine we can but give a few illustrations… Thus, for deafness, the juice of onion has been long recommended, and for chilblains, a Derbyshire cure is to thrash them with holly, **10** while in some places the juice of the leek mixed with cream is held in repute. To exterminate warts a host of plants have been recommended; the juice of the dandelion being in favor in the Midland counties, whereas in the North, one has but to hang a snail on a thorn, and as the poor creature wastes away the warts will disappear. In Leicestershire the ash is employed, and in many places the **15** elder is considered efficacious. Another old remedy is to prick the wart with a gooseberry thorn passed through a wedding-ring; and according to a Cornish belief, the first blackberry seen will banish warts. Watercress laid against warts was formerly said to drive them away. A rustic specific for whooping-cough in Hampshire is to drink new milk out of a cup made of the variegated holly; while **20** in Sussex the excrescence found on the briar, and popularly known as "robin red-breast's cushion," is in demand. In consumption and diseases of the lungs, St. Fabian's nettle, the crocus, the betony, and horehound, have long been in request…

For depression, thyme was recommended, and a Manx preservative against **25** all kinds of infectious diseases is ragwort. The illustrations we have given above show in how many ways plants have been in demand as popular curatives. And although an immense amount of superstition has been interwoven with folk-medicine, there is a certain amount of truth in the many remedies which for centuries have been, with more or less success, employed by the peasantry, both **30** at home and abroad.

Passage 2:

Excerpt from "Homeopathy: Real Medicine or Empty Promises?"
by Isadora Stehlin

Some of the medicines of homeopathy evoke positive images—chamomile, marigold, daisy, onion. But even some of Mother Nature's cruelest creations—poison ivy, mercury, arsenic, pit viper venom, hemlock—are part of homeopathic care.   35

Homeopathy is a medical theory and practice that developed in reaction to the bloodletting, blistering, purging, and other harsh procedures of conventional medicine as it was practiced more than 200 years ago. Remedies made from many sources, including plants, minerals or animals, are prescribed based on both a person's symptoms and personality. Patients receiving homeopathic care   40 frequently feel worse before they get better because homeopathic medicines often stimulate, rather than suppress, symptoms. This seeming reversal of logic is a relevant part of homeopathy because symptoms are viewed as the body's effort to restore health…

In the late 1700s, the most popular therapy for most ailments was   45 bloodletting. Some doctors had so much faith in bleeding that they were willing to remove up to four-fifths of the patient's blood. Other therapies of choice included blistering—placing caustic or hot substances on the skin to draw out infections—and administering dangerous chemicals [or plants] to induce vomiting or purge the bowels. Massive doses of a mercury-containing drug   50 called calomel cleansed the bowels, but at the same time caused teeth to loosen, hair to fall out, and other symptoms of acute mercury poisoning.

Samuel Hahnemann, a German physician disenchanted with these methods, began to develop a theory based on three principles: the law of similars, the minimum dose, and the single remedy.   55

The word homeopathy is derived from the Greek words for like (homoios) and suffering (pathos). With the law of similars, Hahnemann theorized that if a large amount of a substance causes certain symptoms in a healthy person, smaller amounts of the same substance can treat those symptoms in someone who is ill. The basis of his theory took shape after a strong dose of the malaria   60 treatment quinine caused his healthy body to develop symptoms similar to ones caused by the disease. He continued to test his theory on himself as well as family and friends with different herbs, minerals and other substances. He called these experiments "provings."…

FDA Consumer magazine (December 1996)

7. Unlike the author in Passage 2, the author of Passage 1 develops the material by relying on
   A. medical studies and surveys.
   B. exposition and theory.
   C. historic background and secondary sources.
   D. queries and responses.
   E. anecdotes and medicinal traditions.

8. In the last line of Passage 2, the author says that Hahnemann called his experiments "provings," implying that
   A. he conducted the experiments to confirm what he already believed to be true from his past experiences.
   B. Hahnemann wanted to forestall any critics of his new methodology of natural healing.
   C. family and friends needed to be reassured that being guinea pigs for his ideas was fairly safe.
   D. he wanted to use scientific language for his experiments, like the word "proof" in mathematic theorems.
   E. each of the three principals of his theory had to be proven separately.

9. Which of the following best describes the difference between Passages 1 and 2?
   A. Passage 1 lists cures that are not plant based, such as warts being cured by drying up a snail, while Passage 2 mentions plant cures only.
   B. Passage 1 simply gives the name of a plant and what it cures, and credits superstition for healing, while Passage 2 describes the methodology of a specific natural healing process.
   C. Passage 1 negatively assesses superstitions surrounding the use of plants instead of medicines, while Passage 2 is positive in its view of using poisonous plants to cure illnesses.
   D. Passage 1 describes how natural elements, including plants, can harm healthy people, but used in small amounts plants can cure, while Passage 2 gives a general overview of beneficial plants.
   E. Passage 1 examines how using plants as medicines has changed over time, while Passage 2 relates the historic value of plants as curative agents.

10. In the first line of Passage 2, "evoke" most nearly means
    A. extract.   B. deduce.   C. envision.   D. conjure.   E. extort.

Chapter 4
Interpreting Literature—

Literary—or creative—passages in the SAT Critical Reading section require both **understanding** and **interpretation** on your part. **Understanding** the passage comes from carefully reading the passage and absorbing the main idea its author wants to convey. **Interpreting** a passage comes from close attention to detail, including the passage's tone, the author's *characterization* (or portrayal) of people within the passage; the style of language used, and sometimes even *literary devices* (or style techniques). The combination of these aspects of writing, when properly understood, will provide most of the answers to questions accompanying literary passages on the SAT.

This chapter will look at elements of literature and literary devices as they apply to typical SAT literary passages. **Literary elements—genre, character, theme,** and **mood**—are the innate parts of the structure of a literary work. They are found in all literary works, although the author controls the use and nature of each one. Being able to identify the characteristics of these elements in the passages you read will promote an **understanding** of the passage.

Literary devices—such as **flashback** and **foreshadowing**, **figurative language**, and **irony**—are techniques used entirely at the discretion of the author. Some authors will use a significant number of devices, while others will choose to write in a style that relies more on straightforward plot and description. Generally, however, some form of literary device is used by almost all creative writers. Being able to identify the author's use of literary devices in SAT passages will help in interpreting the details of the passage.

Since a large proportion of SAT questions about fiction passages involve the process of interpreting details through a general understanding of the main idea or theme, this chapter will repeatedly take the reader through that process. It will include several sample passages with questions and discussions about how the answers are gathered, using a basic understanding of literary elements and devices. There will also be instances in which interpretation of certain details will rely on putting together information from the passage and arriving at the most relevant conclusion.

LITERARY ELEMENTS

GENRES AND THEIR USE

While there are numerous genres of literature, for the purposes of the SAT literary selections, the most common genres include essays, nonfiction narratives, fictional narratives, and fiction. The following table reviews the characteristics of these genres.

Essay	A short composition that discusses a single topic, written from the author's personal point of view. An essay will usually present an argument supported by facts and the author's experience.
Sub-genres of the essay include:	
• **Historical essay**	an account of the author's understanding of a particular event in history, including the author's interpretation of events. An author might write a historical narrative about the destruction by the Taliban of sacred Buddhist shrines in the 1990s, with the viewpoint that the world should have acted against the Taliban earlier than it did.
• **Personal essay**	a descriptive account based on experiences in the author's life. An essay for college admission is a form of personal essay. The author might write about the importance of higher education in her life and the obstacles she might have had to overcome, and why she should be given the chance to succeed.
• **Political essay**	an argument on a specific political issue, such as the power of multinational corporations, presenting the author's viewpoint on the issue. NPR airs political essays by liberal commentator Daniel Schorr several times a week, covering current events and how they tie into world trends. He evaluates, from his own perspective, whether situations were handled well or if they could have been treated differently.
• **Social commentary**	a descriptive narrative commenting on a social issue in society, such as the changing role of motherhood in a growing economic environment, and presenting a unique view of the issue or an argument about the issue.

Narrative	*Narrative* means the telling of a story. Narratives differ from essays in that they are more descriptive and less argument-based.
Nonfiction Narrative	
• **Biographical nonfiction**	In SAT passages, **nonfiction narratives** often relate factual events from the author's life in the form of a story. Nonfiction narratives are often biographical in nature. An example of a nonfiction narrative would be a child of a military officer writing a true story of what it was like to live on military bases as a child. The narrative could take the form of a story and contain extensive descriptive language and a plot, but the content is fact.
• **Creative nonfiction**	Creative nonfiction narrative is like biographical narrative in that it is based on fact. However, creative nonfiction narrative is not about the author but is more journalistic in nature, presenting real events and situations in a story form. It gives the presentation of facts a higher degree of readability and interest for the reader. An example of creative nonfiction might be the story of an airline pilot's day in the post-9/11 world. Instead of simply describing what the pilot does on the job, the creative nonfiction narrative might treat the pilot as a character in a story and follow the pilot through the day, including his thoughts, his life before that day, and his feelings. The day would be presented as a story which is actually true.
Fictional Narrative	**A fictional narrative** is a story. It contains plot, characters, setting, action, and dramatic and thematic elements. In SAT passages, fictional narratives are often excerpts taken from novels.

SAT passages are usually taken from the above genres. They lend themselves to nuance, implication, character study, and other elements of literature which are of far more concern in SAT questions than a simple understanding of plot, setting, and events. As stated above, SAT questions test not only understanding but also interpretation of literature; passages with a specific point of view or argument can afford more opportunities for response, inference, and agreement or disagreement by the reader.

Practice 1: Genres and Their Use

Read the passages below and answer the questions following each.

Passage 1

Excerpt from "The Crisis" by Thomas Paine

The heart that feels not now is dead; the blood of his children will curse his cowardice who shrinks back at a time when a little might have saved the whole, and made them happy. I love the man that can smile in trouble, that can gather strength from distress, and grow brave by reflection. 'Tis the business of little minds to shrink; but he whose heart is firm, and whose conscience approves his conduct, will pursue his principles unto death.

My own line of reasoning is to myself as straight and clear as a ray of light. Not all the treasures of the world, so far as I believe, could have induced me to support an offensive war, for I think it murder; but if a thief breaks into my house, burns and destroys my property, and kills or threatens to kill me, or those that are in it, and to "bind me in all cases whatsoever" to his absolute will, am I to suffer it?

1. Which genre best characterizes the passage?

    A. fictional narrative
    C. personal essay
    E. social essay

    B. political essay
    D. nonfiction narrative

2. The author would probably agree with all of the following statements **except**

    A. adversity in life makes a person stronger.

    B. war for the sake of conquest is immoral.

    C. a person with strong principles stays true to those principles.

    D. self-defense justifies war.

    E. people who fail to act at the right time will be understood by future generations.

Passage 2

by W.E.B. Dubois, an African American essayist, written in 1903

The Negro race, like all races, is going to be saved by its exceptional men. The problem of education, then, among Negroes must first of all deal with the Talented Tenth; it is the problem of developing the Best of this race that they may guide the Mass away from the contamination and death of the Worst, in their own and other races. Now the training of men is a difficult and intricate task. Its technique is a matter for educational experts, but its object is for the vision of seers. If we make money the object of man-training, we shall develop money-makers but not necessarily men; if we make technical skill the object of education, we may possess artisans but not, in nature, men. Men we shall have only as we make manhood the object of the work of the schools— intelligence, broad sympathy, knowledge of the world that was and is, and of the relation of men to it—this is the curriculum of that Higher Education which must underlie true life. On this foundation we may build bread winning, skill of hand and quickness of brain, with never a fear lest the child and man mistake the means of living for the object of life.

If this be true—and who can deny it—three tasks lay before me; first to show from the past that the Talented Tenth as they have risen among American Negroes have been worthy of leadership; secondly to show how these men may be educated and developed; and thirdly to show their relation to the Negro problem.

3. In the context of the passage, which is the best interpretation of the following quote from the passage?

    [Education's] technique is a matter for educational experts, but its object is for the vision of seers.

    A. The purpose of education is to train people of vision.
    B. Educational experts are visionaries in the field of "training of men."
    C. There is no point in receiving an education in making money, without vision.
    D. Visionaries make the best teachers in an ideal education.
    E. It takes visionaries, not experts, to determine the highest purpose of education.

4. Which statement best describes the author's point of view regarding education for African Americans in 1903?

    A. The Talented Tenth was one of the greatest dilemmas facing African Americans in 1904.
    B. The most talented of the African American community should become visionaries.
    C. An education which trains men in technical skills should be the right of every individual.
    D. The most promising individuals must be educated, become leaders, and support others.
    E. The challenge facing the Talented Tenth in 1904 was to avoid contamination and death.

CHARACTERS AND CHARACTERIZATION

Both fictional and nonfictional narratives contain characters. While reading an SAT narrative passage, it is important to pay attention to the details in the descriptions and actions of the characters. These details reveal the characters' motivations, feelings, and attitudes, which add to a comprehensive understanding of the text. The two main aspects of characterization are character type and character interaction. The following lists of literary terms are used to refer to types of characters and the elements of character interaction:

Types of Characters	
flat	a one-dimensional character, often a minor one. The reader has limited knowledge about the character which can often be stereotypical. An example of a flat character is Miss Caroline Fisher, the school teacher in *To Kill a Mockingbird*.
round	a multi-dimensional character, often one of the main characters. The reader knows many personality aspects of the character. The reader will usually know the backgrounds, feelings, motivations, and personality traits of the round character. Round characters are well developed characters. They are often the protagonists, such as Jem in *To Kill a Mockingbird*.
static	a character that does not experience change or growth during the time frame of a literary work; at the end of a work, the character is essentially the same as at the beginning of the work. Static and flat characters function to move the plot forward more than to present complex human issues and motivations. Dill and Calpurnia in *To Kill a Mockingbird* are examples of static characters.
dynamic	a character that undergoes significant change or personal growth during the time frame of a literary work. It is often through the dynamic character that the author explores human issues and questions such as courage, jealousy, and the nature of heroism. A dynamic character is usually a round character, because it is necessary to know about the character in order to perceive significant change in her or him. Scout is an example of a dynamic character in *To Kill a Mockingbird*.

Many of the details necessary for answering SAT questions in narrative passages are found in the descriptions of the interactions, relationships, and internal thought processes of the characters. Watch for descriptions of this type. It is very likely you will see a question on the SAT which reads, "The relationship between ____ and ____ can best be described as..."

Following is a summary of some of the most common elements of character interaction.

Character Interaction	
Relationships	The **relationships** between characters are usually the catalysts for change, growth, conflict, and resolution within a narrative. An author may reveal relationships through dialogue, description, action, or the internal thoughts of a character. Without relationship, all characters would be static. Look for parts of passages that reveal characters through relationship with other characters, themselves, and objects.
Motivation	What are the reasons that characters have for acting in a certain way? Reasons are often based on some form of fear or desire. In *Star Wars: Episode III,* both forces provided **motivation** for Anakin Skywalker to go to the Dark Side: the fear of losing his wife in childbirth and the desire to prevent it. Fear does not always mean a quaking of knees. It is often merely a deep motivation to avoid something that threatens happiness. Desire may take the form of a character's longing for home, which causes him to take a journey which brings all forms of adventure.
Conflict	**Conflict** is a major element of character interaction. Through conflict, change is made. Conflict can be internal or external. An **internal conflict** occurs when the character struggles with a problem within himself. An **external conflict** occurs between two characters or between a character and an external force. For example, a narrative about the war in Iraq may involve the character's conflict with the enemy, while he also deals with the fear of being a coward. How characters deal with and solve conflicts reveals the kind of people they are.
Influence	An **influence** is some outside pressure or force that can change the thoughts and actions of a character. A character may draw upon the influence of her experience bringing up a mentally handicapped child to become a successful politician and advocate for parents. In an example from classical literature, the institution of slavery influences Huckleberry Finn's attitude and interactions with his friend Jim until he is able to overcome those influences and see Jim both as a person and a friend. How a character reacts to influences says a great deal about the character.

In literary passages, the author may develop characters through the following techniques:

How Authors Develop Characters	
Description	An author uses **description** to tell how characters look, what they wear, and what their ages are. In *The Secret of the Andes*, Ann Nolan Clark describes the minstrel who comes to visit the protagonist, an Incan boy named Cusi, as "as Indian, with shin-length cotton trousers and a woven cocoa bag." In further describing the minstrel as having the "fierce look of Inca kings," Clark depicts him in a way that not only shows his appearance, but also his history and heritage.
Narration	**Narration** is the telling of a story. A story's narration can come from an unidentified observer, or it might come through a character who tells the story in the first person. In *The Secret of the Andes*, there is an unidentified narrator describing all events as an unidentified observer. In *The Adventures of Huckleberry Finn*, Huck is the narrator and narrates the story in first person.
Dialogue	Through **dialogue** between characters, an author can reveal information about the characters. A sample of dialogue between Cusi and the old man who looks after him illustrates this. In the conversation, Cusi expresses his happiness at seeing people in the valley. The old man remembers that Cusi had not seen people since coming to live with him as a small child. Then he tells Cusi it is time for them to go on a trip and meet other Indians. In this conversation, we learn the situation of a boy who has never really seen people, and we learn how excited he is to finally see some. We also learn about the character of the old man, who cares about Cusi and who knows it is time to let him learn about the world and other people.
Dialect	**Dialect** is used to portray a character's cultural and regional heritage by having him speak in his natural manner. "The Treasure of Lemon Brown" contains a good example of dialect used by the character of Lemon Brown. Notice the way his language contains missing words and non-standard usage when he responds to Greg's doubt about his treasure: "What you mean, *if* I have one? Every man got a treasure. You don't know that, you must be a fool!"
Actions	Sometimes the **actions** of a character speak louder than words to show the character's true self. Saruman the White, the wizard in J.R.R. Tolkien's *The Lord of the Rings*, is the protector of the inhabitants of Middle Earth and Gandalf the Grey's mentor. He should protect Gandalf, but he betrays him for the power promised by Sauron, the evil antagonist. On the other hand, the main characters in O. Henry's "The Gift of the Magi" show positive characteristics through actions. They show their love for each other by placing the happiness of the other before their own.

Practice 2: Characters and Characterization

Read the passages carefully, and answer the questions that follow each.

Passage 1

Exerpt from *The Bostonians* by Henry James

"Olive told me to tell you she hoped you will stay to dinner. And if she said it, she does really hope it."

"Just as I am?" the visitor inquired, presenting himself with rather a work-a-day aspect.

Mrs. Luna glanced at him from head to foot, and gave a little smiling sigh, as if he had been a long sum in addition. And, indeed, he was very long, Basil Ransom, and he even looked a little hard and discouraging, like a column of figures, in spite of the friendly face which he bent upon his hostess's deputy, and which, in its thinness, had a deep dry line, a sort of premature wrinkle, on either side of the mouth. He was tall and lean, and dressed throughout in black; his shirt-collar was low and wide, and the triangle of linen, a little crumpled, exhibited by the opening of his waistcoat, was adorned by a pin containing a small red stone.

In spite of this decoration the young man looked poor—as poor as a young man could look who had such a fine head and such magnificent eyes. Those of Basil Ransom were dark, deep, and glowing; his head had a character of elevation which fairly added to his stature; it was a head to be seen above the level of a crowd, on some judicial bench or political platform, or even on a bronze medal. His forehead was high and broad, and his thick black hair, perfectly straight and glossy, and without any division, rolled back from it in a leonine manner.

These things, the eyes especially, with their smouldering fire, might have indicated that he was to be a great American statesman; or, on the other hand, they might simply have proved that he came from Carolina or Alabama. He came, in fact, from Mississippi, and he spoke very perceptibly with the accent of that country. Mrs. Luna looked up at all this, but saw only a part of it; otherwise she would not have replied in a bantering manner, in answer to his inquiry: "Are you ever different from this?" Mrs. Luna was familiar—intolerably familiar.

1. The author develops the main character of the passage primarily through which of the following characterization techniques?

   A. description
   B. dialect
   C. actions
   D. dialogue
   E. narration

2. The author's references to the character's eyes in the second and third paragraphs most likely imply that

    A. he is an angry man.
    B. he should not be trusted.
    C. he is concealing a mysterious past.
    D. he carries with him some pain from past experiences.
    E. his character has depth and passion not yet revealed.

3. The last line, describing Mrs. Luna's attitude and behavior, indicates which of the following statements about Basil Ransom's character?

    A. He is a southern gentleman embarrassed by her attitude.
    B. He accepts her assumptions about him.
    C. He is uncomfortable with her rudeness.
    D. He is a simple man, confused by her attitude.
    E. He resents her remarks, which portray him as incapable of change.

THEME

SAT reading questions which call upon an understanding of theme may be worded a,s "The main idea of the passage is..." or "This passage is about..." or "According to the passage, which statement about ___ is true?" In order to answer this type of question, you should understand the overall message or idea the passage conveys.

Themes are deeper meanings than main ideas in passages (see Chapter 3: Reading Comprehension). While all passages, including, for instance, a technical passage on how microchips work, have main ideas, in literary and narrative passages, a theme explores human issues, experience, and the meaning of experience. Themes are usually universal: they are common truths that most people can relate to.

Common Themes	
Love	a first love is unmatched, love can transform us
Change	change is inevitable, change is challenging, an end can mean a beginning
Growing Up	losing a childhood means gaining adulthood, there are some pains of growing up that all must experience
Intolerance	intolerance comes from ignorance, intolerance can have tragic consequences
Loss	wondering what happens after death, losses can help people to mature

There are numerous themes to be found in the short and long passages of the SAT. Many are not as universal as the ones listed above but are more specific to the passage. Many passages can also include more than one theme. For instance, a narrative about a mother rereading the letters of a son who has left home may reveal themes about regret, pride, and hope at the same time.

Themes are not usually stated in a literary work; the reader must infer the theme by understanding all the details in the work. Here are two tips for how to determine the theme of a literary work:

1. Look at the lessons the main character learns throughout the passage. How has the character changed throughout the work? Has the character learned anything new? Often the truth revealed to a character is the same truth the author wants to reveal to the reader.

2. Look at the conflicts in the passage and how they are resolved. A passage with the theme of love may involve the conflict of overcoming separation: one theme in several of Shakespeare's plays is the triumph of youth and love over age. While elders and authorities try to obstruct young people's love, the love and idealism of the youth wins over the fears and prejudices of the old.

Practice 3: Theme

Read the passage carefully, and answer the questions which follow it.

Passage 1

Excerpt from "The First Snowfall" by Guy de Maupassant

She recalls the past. She had been married, four years ago, to a Norman gentleman. He was a strong young man, bearded, healthy-looking, with wide shoulders, narrow mind, and joyous disposition.

They had been united through financial motives which she knew nothing about. She would willingly have said No. She said Yes, with a movement of the head, in order not to thwart her father and mother. She was a Parisian, gay, and full of the joy of living.

 Her husband brought her home to his Norman chateau. It was a huge stone building surrounded by tall trees of great age. A high clump of pine trees shut out the view in front. On the right, an opening in the trees presented a view of the plain, which stretched out in an unbroken level as far as the distant, farmsteads. A cross-road passed before the gate and led to the high road three kilometres away.

Oh! she recalls everything, her arrival, her first day in her new abode, and her isolated life afterward.

When she stepped out of the carriage, she glanced at the old building and laughingly exclaimed:

"It does not look cheerful!"

Her husband began to laugh in his turn, and replied:

"Pooh! We'll get used to it! You'll see. I never feel bored in it, for my part."

That day they passed their time in embracing each other, and she did not find it too long. This lasted fully a month. The days passed one after the other in insignificant yet absorbing occupations. She learned the value and the importance of the little things of life. She knew that people can interest themselves in the price of eggs, which cost a few centimes more or less according to the seasons.

It was summer. She went to the fields to see the men harvesting. The brightness of the sunshine found an echo in her heart.

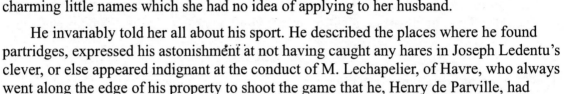

The autumn came. Her husband went out shooting. He started in the morning with his two dogs Medor and Mirza. She remained alone, without grieving, moreover, at Henry's absence. She was very fond of him, but she did not miss him. When he returned home, her affection was especially bestowed on the dogs. She took care of them every evening with a mother's tenderness, caressed them incessantly, gave them a thousand charming little names which she had no idea of applying to her husband.

He invariably told her all about his sport. He described the places where he found partridges, expressed his astonishment at not having caught any hares in Joseph Ledentu's clever, or else appeared indignant at the conduct of M. Lechapelier, of Havre, who always went along the edge of his property to shoot the game that he, Henry de Parville, had started.

She replied: "Yes, indeed! it is not right," thinking of something else all the while.

1. The main idea of this passage is

   A. the grief of a widow remembering the happy years of her marriage.
   B. the idyllic life of the aristocratic life during the Victorian era.
   C. the value of hunting and outdoor activities to the health of a marriage.
   D. a woman's memory of a lonely marriage to a self-absorbed man.
   E. the importance of a man's protection of his property and the game on it.

2. Judging from reading this passage, which of the following could be one of the themes of this work?

   A. When they are married, people always think more about their spouse than about themselves.
   B. Married couples always share their experiences and take part in one another's interests.
   C. Though two people are not passionately in love, they can live together in relative harmony.
   D. A husband may become jealous of his wife's attention to the pets in the household.
   E. Newlyweds often do not know anything about how to behave in marriage.

3. What does the author imply in the following sentence from the second paragraph (reproduced below)?

   They had been united through financial motives which she knew nothing about.

   A. The wife was forced to marry the husband due to poverty.
   B. The husband had stood to gain a large dowry for marrying the wife.
   C. The life she accepted with the husband had little to do with her own wishes.
   D. The wife worked to alleviate the financial concerns of her husband and parents.
   E. She married her husband in order to become rich.

LITERARY DEVICES

SAT narrative passages do not often test specifically the many forms of literary devices. This kind of testing of facts and details from the high school English curriculum is less the purpose of the SAT reading section than the testing of comprehension, attention to content details, the ability to infer meaning, and the ability to draw conclusions: in other words, the ability to think critically about what you read.

At the same time, literary devices are used in most narrative literature, whether subtly or overtly, and a review of some of the major forms of these devices will promote understanding of the passages. This section will look at the literary devices of **flashback, foreshadowing, figurative language**, and **irony**.

FLASHBACK AND FORESHADOWING

A **flashback** is a turn of events in a story line which brings the reader back to a scene or event that happened before the story began. It may also be provided through dialogue between two of the characters. The purpose of a flashback is not merely to add extra information to a story, but to help the reader better understand the present circumstances of the story. It will also help the reader to understand characters by revealing their backgrounds and earlier experiences.

An example of flashback can be found in the movie *Spider-Man 2*. In one of the later scenes in the movie, Peter Parker sits at the dining room table with his aunt and tells her the real story of her husband's death. The story implies that Peter may have been to blame for the death. This flashback scene serves to illuminate Peter's present motivations for his quest to bring more justice and safety into the world. It also reveals his character, illustrating that he has the courage to tell the truth, even though it hurts his aunt and threatens their relationship.

Foreshadowing is another way of impacting the flow of time in a story. Foreshadowing takes place when an author includes certain details in one part of the story which hint at events to come. These details are sometimes subtle and not recognized until the whole story is read. In other works, they immediately affect the reader as clues to predict what might happen later in the story.

Like flashback, foreshadowing can be created through dialogue, description, or action. At times, it may be overt. A description of a meaningful glance or a sudden reaction by one character at the mention of the name of another character will indicate that the relationship and actions between the two will probably be a significant part of the plot.

Sometimes foreshadowing is more subtle, taking the form of symbolism. A character dropping and shattering a treasured object before a special event may foreshadow disaster or distress in the subsequent events. An example is found in Washington Irving's "The Specter Bridegroom." In this story, a mysterious knight arrives at a castle just before a marriage feast. At first, his identity is unknown, but he is described in great detail by the author: riding a magnificent black horse, a common symbol of death. Recognizing this detail, a reader may glimpse the likelihood of future events in the story.

FIGURATIVE LANGUAGE

Figurative language is a creative way to produce effective descriptions and images. As an example, think about the phrase "There were more people there than you could say grace over!" This expression conveys the simple idea that there were a lot of people in a certain place. But it also expresses that idea in a comically ambiguous way. It begs the question, "What is the maximum number of people someone can say grace over?" Ironically, since "grace" is supposedly based on thought, an immeasurable entity, what would it have to do with numbers? It is the irony and humor in this figurative expression which gives it effectiveness. It lends color, image, humor, and delight to an otherwise straightforward account of a large group of people.

The following table lists some of the common forms of figurative language.

Sound Devices	**Sound devices**, as the name implies, are literary devices that add a particular sound to the text, which can create a mood or appeal to the senses. Sound devices include **alliteration**, **onomatopoeia**, **rhyme**, and **rhythm**.
• Alliteration	**Alliteration** is the repetition of the same consonant sounds in lines of poetry or prose. Examples: (1) "Droning a drowsy syncopated tune,"–Langston Hughes (2) "I like to see it lap the miles, / And lick the valleys up," –Emily Dickinson (repetition of "l" sounds).
• Onomatopoeia	An **onomatopoeia** is a word whose sound suggests its meaning. Examples: (1) splash, buzz, hiss, boom (2) "The *moan* of doves in immemorial elms; / And *murmuring* of innumerable bees," –Alfred, Lord Tennyson.
• Rhyme	**Rhyme** is the pairing of words that have the same sound at the end of lines of poetry. Examples: (1) "The Angel that presided o'er my birth / Said, "Little creature, formed of joy and mirth, / Go, love without the help of anything on earth." –William Blake
• Rhythm	**Rhythm** is the arrangement of stressed and unstressed syllables into a pattern. While rhythm is almost always found in poetry, quality prose writing also involves regular patterns that appeal to the reader. Read the following example out loud: "She wept at once, with sudden, wild abandonment, in her sister's arms." – Kate Chopin

Analogy	An **analogy** is the technique of describing something unfamiliar or difficult to explain by comparing it with something familiar. **Metaphors** and **similes** are forms of analogy.
Simile	A comparison between two otherwise dissimilar things using the word "like" or the word "as" to make the comparison. Example: "You're *like* a leaf that the wind blows from one gutter to another." – Jeff Bailey (played by Robert Mitchum), in the movie *Out of the Past*: he directly compares the woman who betrayed him to a leaf moving amont the gutters. (2) Free *as* a bird.
Metaphor	A comparison between two unlike objects or events *without* using the words "like" or "as." Instead, the qualities given to one object **imply** its similarity to another. Example: "Years of strip mining had left a network of permanent scars on the landscape outside of town." Without directly stating it, this metaphor compares the landscape to skin, since it is the function of skin, not earth, to scar.
Allusion	**Allusion** is a reference to a well-known place, literary or art work, famous person, or historical event. Today these references are often related to current pop culture. The television series "The Gilmore Girls" is known for its dialogue replete with allusions. In order for an allusion to work, the reader must be familiar with the work or item being referred to. Some examples: "The gift turned out to be more like a Trojan horse." (allusion to Greek legend) "When it came to giving gifts, she acted like Scrooge." (allusion to Dickens character)
Hyperbole	**Hyperbole** is the use of exaggeration to create an effect. Examples: (1) I just about died when I found out I had the lead role! (2) I must have been to a million soccer games this year! (3) I've driven my way around the world ten times.
Understatement	**Understatement** is the opposite of hyperbole, a way of stressing the importance or impact of an issue or event by minimizing the expression of it. For instance, a person who just won the Nobel Prize in Physics might remark at the end of the day, "It's been a good day."

Imagery	**Imagery** is the use of any words that evoke sensations of sight, hearing, touch, smell, or taste. For example, in *The Mists of Avalon*, Marion Zimmer Bradley describes a character's familiarity with the moon. This character "...knew the moon's changes as if they ran in the tides of her own blood."
Personification	**Personification** is giving human qualities to something not human. For example, in Mary Shelley's *Frankenstein*, the main character refuses to comply with the monster's demands at one point, saying, "and no torture shall ever extort a consent from me." Shelley is personifying torture as a being capable of extortion.
Symbol	A **symbol** is an object, person, place, or action that has a meaning in itself and that also represents a meaning beyond itself, such as a quality, an attitude, a belief, or a value. For example, in the play *A Raisin in the Sun*, Mama carefully tends to her favorite houseplant throughout the sad events of the play. Her plant symbolizes hope in the midst of tragedy.

IRONY

Irony is one of the most ubiquitous elements of both literature and life and yet one of the most complex concepts to describe. Definitions alone cannot explain why irony is the compelling and effective literary device that it is. Why should contrasts in ideas be a notable form of literature? Much of the power of irony can be felt only in context. "You have to be there." The following table provides examples of four kinds of irony.

Verbal irony	**Verbal irony** is incongruity between what is *said* and what is commonly *understood to be true*. The character who is speaking knows that he or she is saying the opposite of what is understood, perhaps to point out something that some people—but not others—may understand. **Sarcasm** is a harsh form of verbal irony, designed to hurt or belittle another person. For example, "If you're such an expert, why don't you run the class!"
Dramatic irony	**Dramatic irony** is also spoken, but the discrepancy comes from the speaker not realizing that something incongruous has been said. Often, the truth of the character's statement is revealed elsewhere in the story. An example comes from Shakespeare's *Othello*, in which the protagonist Othello calls another character "honest Iago." The irony, which the reader/audience sees, is that Othello does not yet know that Iago is plotting against him and is, in truth, the least honest of men.

Situational irony	**Situational irony** is a discrepancy of situation, a difference between what is expected to happen and what actually happens. Situational irony defies logical cause/effect outcomes. An example of situational irony occurs in an episode of the television series "The West Wing," when one character spends much of the episode trying to prove to the others that it is possible to stand an egg on end during the Equinox. The other characters emphatically deny the possibility. At the end of the episode, the character succeeds in the seemingly impossible feat, but it is at the only time in the entire program in which no one is there to see it.
Tragic irony	**Tragic irony** occurs, as one would guess, in tragedies. Tragic irony can involve verbal, dramatic, and situational irony, with the difference that the effects of the irony are very sad, possibly catastrophic. Stephen Crane's *Maggie, Girl of the Streets* contains tragic irony. The main character, Maggie, is described early in the novel as a rare flower blooming in the squalor of the ghetto. While she is the only character capable of love and goodness, she also becomes the only one incapable of surviving the hatred and cruelty of that same ghetto.

Practice 4: Figurative Language and Irony

Read the following two passages and answer the questions that follow.

Passage 1

Excerpt from "In the Spring" by Guy de Maupassant

My neighbor raised her eyes again, and this time, as I was still looking at her, she smiled decidedly. She was charming, and in her passing glance I saw a thousand things, which I had hitherto been ignorant of, for I perceived unknown depths, all the charm of tenderness, all the poetry which we dream of, all the happiness which we are continually in search of. I felt an insane longing to open my arms and to carry her off somewhere, so as to whisper the sweet music of words of love into her ears.

I was just about to address her when somebody touched me on the shoulder, and as I turned round in some surprise, I saw an ordinary-looking man, who was neither young nor old, and who gazed at me sadly.

"I should like to speak to you," he said.

I made a grimace, which he no doubt saw, for he added:

"It is a matter of importance."

I got up, therefore, and followed him to the other end of the boat and then he said:

"Monsieur, when winter comes, with its cold, wet and snowy weather, your doctor says to you constantly: 'Keep your feet warm, guard against chills, colds, bronchitis, rheumatism and pleurisy.'

"Then you are very careful, you wear flannel, a heavy greatcoat and thick shoes, but all this does not prevent you from passing two months in bed. But when spring returns, with its leaves and flowers, its warm, soft breezes and its smell of the fields, all of which causes you vague disquiet and causeless emotion, nobody says to you:

"'Monsieur, beware of love! It is lying in ambush everywhere; it is watching for you at every corner; all its snares are laid, all its weapons are sharpened, all its guiles are prepared! Beware of love! Beware of love! It is more dangerous than brandy, bronchitis or pleurisy! It never forgives and makes everybody commit irreparable follies.'

"Yes, monsieur, I say that the French Government ought to put large public notices on the walls, with these words: 'Return of spring. French citizens, beware of love!' just as they put: 'Beware of paint.'"

"However, as the government will not do this, I must supply its place, and I say to you: 'Beware of love!' for it is just going to seize you, and it is my duty to inform you of it, just as in Russia they inform any one that his nose is frozen."

I was much astonished at this individual, and assuming a dignified manner, I said:

"Really, monsieur, you appear to me to be interfering in a matter which is no concern of yours."

He made an abrupt movement and replied:

"Ah! monsieur, monsieur! If I see that a man is in danger of being drowned at a dangerous spot, ought I to let him perish? So just listen to my story and you will see why I ventured to speak to you like this."

1. The story of an older man attempting to rescue a young man, from what he sees as a danger as serious as drowning, is an example of

   A. situational irony.   C. tragic irony.
   B. verbal irony.   D. dramatic irony.

2. The sentence "I say that the French Government ought to put large public notices on the walls, with these words: 'Return of spring. French citizens, beware of love!'" is an example of

   A. situational irony.   C. tragic irony.
   B. verbal irony.   D. dramatic irony.

Passage 2

Excerpt from "The First Snowfall" by Guy de Maupassant

The winter came, the Norman winter, cold and rainy. The endless floods of rain came down the tin slates of the great gabled roof, rising like a knife blade toward the sky. The roads seemed like rivers of mud, the country a plain of mud, and no sound could be heard save that of water falling; no movement could be seen save the whirling flight of crows that settled down like a cloud on a field and then hurried off again.

About four o'clock, the army of dark, flying creatures came and perched in the tall beeches at the left of the chateau, emitting deafening cries. During nearly an hour, they flew from tree top to tree top, seemed to be fighting, croaked, and made a black disturbance in the gray branches. She gazed at them each evening with a weight at her heart, so deeply was she impressed by the lugubrious melancholy of the darkness falling on the deserted country.

Then she rang for the lamp, and drew near the fire. She burned heaps of wood without succeeding in warming the spacious apartments reeking with humidity. She was cold all day long, everywhere, in the drawing-room, at meals, in her own apartment. It seemed to her she was cold to the marrow of her bones. Her husband only came in to dinner; he was always out shooting, or else he was superintending sowing the seed, tilling the soil, and all the work of the country.

3. All the following phrases from the passage can be seen as a foreshadowing of death **except**
   A. the roads seemed like rivers of mud
   B. it seemed to her she was cold to the marrow of her bones.
   C. the whirling flight of crows that settled down like a cloud on a field
   D. the lugubrious melancholy of the darkness falling on the deserted country
   E. the tin slates of the great gabled roof, rising like a knife blade toward the sky.

4. In the second paragraph the phrase "the army of dark, flying creatures" is an example of
   A. tragic irony.   C. hyperbole.   E. personification.
   B. dramatic irony.   D. alliteration.

CHAPTER 4 REVIEW

Read the passages carefully and answer the questions which follow each.

Passage 1

Excerpt from *Ruth Hall* by Fanny Fern

... Ruth remembered how she used to wish she were beautiful—not that she might be admired, but that she might be loved. But Ruth was "very plain,"—so her brother Hyacinth told her, and "awkward," too; she had heard that ever since she could remember; and the recollection of it dyed her cheek with blushes, whenever a stranger made his appearance in the home circle.

The world smiled on her brother Hyacinth. He was handsome, and gifted. He could win fame, and what was better, love. Ruth wished he would love her a little. She often used to steal into his room and "right" his papers, when the stupid housemaid had displaced them; and often she would prepare him a tempting little lunch, and carry it to his room, on his return from his morning walk; but Hyacinth would only say, "Oh, it is you, Ruth, is it? I thought it was Bridget"; and go on reading his newspaper.

After her mother's death, Ruth was sent to boarding-school, where she shared a room with four strange girls who lay awake all night, telling the most extraordinary stories, and ridiculing Ruth for being such an old maid that she could not see "where the laugh came in." Equally astonishing to the unsophisticated Ruth was the demureness with which they would bend over their books when the pale, meek-eyed widow, employed as duenna, went the rounds after tea, to see if each inmate was preparing the next day's lessons, and the coolness with which they would jump up, on her departure, put on their bonnets and shawls, and slip out at the side-street door to meet expectant lovers; and when the pale widow went the rounds again at nine o'clock, she would find them demurely seated, just where she left them, apparently busily conning their lessons! Ruth wondered if all girls were as mischievous, and if fathers and mothers ever stopped to think what companions their daughters would have for room-mates and bed-fellows, when they sent them away from home.

In the all-absorbing love affairs which were constantly going on between the young ladies of Madame Moreau's school and their respective admirers, Ruth took no interest; and on the occasion of the unexpected reception of a bouquet, from a smitten swain, accompanied by a copy of amatory verses, Ruth crimsoned to her temples and burst into tears, that anyone could be found so heartless as to burlesque the "awkward" Ruth.

Simple child! She was unconscious that, in the freedom of that atmosphere where a "prophet out of his own country is honored," her lithe form had rounded into symmetry and grace, her slow step had become light and elastic, her eye bright, her smile winning, and her voice soft and melodious. Other bouquets, other notes, and glances of involuntary admiration from passers-by, at length opened her eyes to the fact, that she was "plain, awkward Ruth" no longer. Eureka! She had arrived at the first epoch in a young girl's life —she had found out her power! Her manners became assured and self-possessed. She, Ruth, could inspire love! Life became dear to her. There was something worth living for —something to look forward to.

When Ruth had been a year at school, her elegant brother Hyacinth came to see her. Ruth dashed down her books, and bounded down three stairs at a time, to meet him; for she loved him, poor child, just as well as if he were worth loving.

1. Which statement best describes the relationship between Ruth and her brother?

   A. Ruth and Hyacinth have a warm familial relationship.
   B. Ruth and Hyacinth do not understand each other and have little in common.
   C. There is love between them, but Victorian society discouraged displays of affection.
   D. Ruth admires and loves her brother, who is critical and condescending towards her.
   E. Ruth and Hyacinth both harbor resentment towards each other.

2. In the sixth paragraph, the phrase "... in the freedom of that atmosphere, where a 'prophet out of his own country is honored,'" is an example of
   A. dramatic irony.   C. allusion.   E. analogy.
   B. onomatopoeia.   D. hyperbole.

3. In the last line, the phrase "for she loved him, poor child, just as well as if he were worth loving" is an example of which literary element?
   A. character development   C. personification   E. flashback
   B. symbolism   D. foreshadowing

Passage 2

Excerpt from "The Bee" by Mark Twain

During substantially the whole of her short life of five or six years the queen [bee] lives in the Egyptian darkness and stately seclusion of the royal apartments, with none about her but plebeian servants, who give her empty lip-affection in place of the love which her heart hungers for; who spy upon her in the interest of her waiting heirs, and report and exaggerate her defects and deficiencies to them; who fawn upon her and flatter her to her face and slander her behind her back; who grovel before her in the day of her power and forsake her in her age and weakness.

There she sits, friendless, upon her throne through the long night of her life, cut off from the consoling sympathies and sweet companionship and loving endearments which she craves, by the gilded barriers of her awful rank; a forlorn exile in her own house and home, weary object of formal ceremonies and machine-made worship, winged child of the sun, native to the free air and the blue skies and the flowery fields, doomed by the splendid accident of her birth to trade this priceless heritage for a black captivity, a tinsel grandeur, and a loveless life, with shame and insult at the end and a cruel death—and condemned by the human instinct in her to hold the bargain valuable!

After the queen, the personage next in importance in the hive is the virgin. The virgins are fifty thousand or one hundred thousand in number, and they are the workers, the laborers. No work is done, in the hive or out of it, save by them. The males do not work, the queen does no work, unless laying eggs is work, but it does not seem so to me. There are only two million of them, anyway, and all of five months to finish the contract in. The distribution of work in a hive is as cleverly and elaborately specialized as it is in a vast American machine-shop or factory.

4.   In the first paragraph, the expression "Egyptian darkness" is
   A.   an allusion to the fact that night is darker in Egypt than anywhere else.
   B.   a color name for black copyrighted by commercial crayon companies.
   C.   an implication that the country of Egypt lives in darkness of ignorance.
   D.   an allusion to the Egypt as the land of six months of darkness.
   E.   a reference to the bible story of the plague of darkness upon Egypt.

5.   The expression "a forlorn exile in her own house and home" is an example of
   A.   understatement.
   B.   situational irony.
   C.   symbol.

    D.   simile.

    E.   analogy.

6.   The sentence "There are only two million of them, anyway, and all of five months to finish the contract in" is an example of

    A.   imagery.

    B.   rhythm.

    C.   hyperbole.

    D.   metaphor.

    E.   understatement.

SAT Reading Preparation
Practice Test 1

Section 1

24 Questions

Time – 25 minutes

Directions: For each question in this section, select the best answer from among the given choices.

Each sentence below has one or two blanks, each blank indicating that something has been omitted. Beneath the sentence are five choices, labeled A through E. Choose the word or combination of words that, when placed in the sentence, *best* fits the sentence's meaning.

Example: Bob worried it was only a matter of time before Katie_____; she'd been enthusiastic about the plan yesterday, but he expected her to feel differently once she gave the idea serious _____.

 A. wavered… decision
 B. obliged… hesitation
 C. demurred… consideration
 D. argued… rethinking
 E. exited… reconciliation

The correct answer is *C*.

---

1. We all knew it would be a while. Ten feet away, another reporter _____, this one _____ picking pieces of lint off his brown wool suit.

   A. paused...actually

   B. yawned...frantically

   C. lingered...meticulously

   D. sighed...carelessly

   E. attended...compulsively

2. He drove by the giant reservoir as the landscape opened up to reveal a vast _____ of water on his right-hand side.

   A. array

   B. sweep

   C. space

   D. display

   E. expanse

3. She is the ultimate _____ mother, proud of her godchild's _____.

   A. liberal...characteristics

   B. tolerant... stinginess

   C. derelict...heritage

   D. surrogate...accomplishments

   E. unconventional...weaknesses

4. She was still in her business attire from that morning, and it was difficult to _____ around the deck boards in heels.

   A. engage

   B. span

   C. tread

   D. traverse

   E. maneuver

5. Her _____ was beginning to slip, her voice starting to rise _____.

   A. equilibrium... curiously

   B. composure... angrily

   C. aplomb...nervously

   D. nonchalance... anxiously

   E. posture... hopefully

6. In back of the old house was a huge abandoned barn, a faded _____ of what the property once was.

   A. remnant

   B. figment

   C. vintage

   D. depreciation

   E. derivative

7. He waved his hand tilted back at the wrist, a cool gesture meant to be _____ to us, as he walked towards the others.

   A. disruptive

   B. pejorative

   C. disingenuous

   D. submissive

   E. dismissive

8. An agreement is already in place for the King to _____ the throne in favor of his brother, the Duke.

   A. abdicate

   B. adjudicate

   C. altercate

   D. ambulate

   E. ameliorate

The passages below are followed by questions based on content. Questions following a pair of related passages may also ask how the passages relate to one another. Answer the questions below on the basis of what is *stated* or *implied* in the passages as well as any introductory material provided.

Questions 9–10 are based on this passage:

In February of 1898, an insurrection broke out on the island of Cuba. Cubans nationals had become increasingly dissatisfied with Spanish rule. The United States (5)had a great deal invested in Cuba and sided with the insurgents. As the insurgency continued, US domestic animosity toward Spain increased as sensationalist purveyors of "yellow journalism" such as (10)William Randolph Hearst further incited the anger of the American public. When the *U.S.S. Maine* was sunk in Havana Harbor under mysterious circumstances, public outrage increased (15)pressure on President McKinley to take action. Despite a personal desire for a peaceful resolution, McKinley sent a request to Congress for the use of military force in Cuba. Once at war with Spain, the (20)US moved to take control of the Philippines, half a world away in the South Pacific, as well.

9. Which of the following can be inferred from the above passage?
   A. The United States wanted to conquer all of the South Pacific.
   B. President McKinley was a pacifist.
   C. Spain also wanted war as an excuse to invade Florida.
   D. Newspaper coverage urged the American people to want war.
   E. William Randolph Hearst wanted to see Spain conquered.

10. The author's attitude towards "yellow journalism" could be described best as
    A. openly approving.
    B. objective curiosity.
    C. bitter acrimony.
    D. measured disdain.
    E. vague worry.

Questions 11–12 are based on this passage

The manta ray is the largest of all rays and reaches a maximum body weight of 3000 lbs. The ray is found throughout the world's tropical seas, most commonly in (5)or around food-providing coral reefs. In most species, the manta is commonly colored black above its dorsal plane (the horizontal line passing through a given animal's middle) and white on its rubbery (10)belly, but some have dark blue shading on their "backs." A manta's eyes sit atop its head, with its mouth and smelling nostrils at its snub front. The manta uses two sets of five gills to breathe, in (15)conjunction with small holes called *spiracles* which sit just behind its eyes. The manta can actually alternate which spiracle is used for inhaling and which for exhaling. Of all the forms of exotic sea (20)life, the manta ranks as one of the most intriguing. Divers, too, appreciate the manta, whose sleek form and effortless glide through the water demonstrate marine life at its most elegant.

11. The author would most likely agree with which of the following ideas about manta rays?

    A.   Manta rays make good pets.

    B.   A manta is a welcome sight to novice divers.

    C.   Scientists should pursue further study of the manta ray.

    D.   Mantas eat only what they can find on coral reefs.

    E.   Mantas should not swim around coral reefs.

12. In line 21, the word "appreciate" mostly closely means that

    A.   divers put a monetary value on manta hide.

    B.   scientists believe mantas are growing in popularity.

    C.   divers respect and admire the manta's swimming style.

    D.   divers are grateful the manta doesn't eat them.

    E.   mantas only want to help divers.

Questions 13–24 are based on this passage:

Excerpt from *Jane Eyre*, by Charlotte Brontë

Jane Eyre chronicles the life of a young orphan girl as she grows up in the Victorian age. In this excerpt, Jane is a young woman reflecting on her life as a governess (a private tutor in both academics and etiquette) at an English manor.

The promise of a smooth career, which my first calm introduction to Thornfield Hall seemed to pledge, was not belied on a longer acquaintance with the place and its inmates. Mrs. Fairfax (5)turned out to be what she appeared, a placid-tempered, kind-natured woman, of competent education and average intelligence. My pupil was a lively child, who had been spoilt and indulged, and therefore was sometimes (10)wayward; but as she was committed entirely to my care, and no injudicious interference from any quarter ever thwarted my plans for her improvement, she soon forgot her little freaks, and became obedient and teachable. She had no (15)great talents, no marked traits of character, no peculiar development of feeling or taste which raised her one inch above the ordinary level of childhood; but neither had she any deficiency or vice which sunk her below it. She (20)made reasonable progress, entertained for me a vivacious, though perhaps not very profound, affection; and by her simplicity, gay prattle, and efforts to please, inspired me, in return, with a degree of attachment sufficient to (25)make us both content in each other's society.

This, par parenthèse, will be thought cool language by persons who entertain solemn doctrines about the angelic nature of children, and the duty of those charged with their (30)education to conceive for them an idolatrous devotion: but I am not writing to flatter parental egotism, to echo cant, or prop up humbug; I am merely telling the truth. I felt a conscientious solicitude for Adèle's welfare and progress, and (35)a quiet liking for her little self: just as I cherished towards Mrs. Fairfax a thankfulness for her kindness, and a pleasure in her society proportionate to the tranquil regard she had for me, and the moderation of her mind and (40)character.

Anybody may blame me who likes, when I add further, that, now and then, when I took a walk by myself in the grounds; when I went down to the gates and looked through them along the (45)road; or when, while Adèle played with her nurse, and Mrs. Fairfax made jellies in the storeroom, I climbed the three staircases, raised the trap-door of the attic, and having reached the leads, looked out afar over sequestered field and

(50)hill, and along dim sky-line—that then I longed for a power of vision which might overpass that limit; which might reach the busy world, towns, regions full of life I had heard of but never seen—that then I desired more of (55)practical experience than I possessed; more of intercourse with my kind, of acquaintance with variety of character, than was here within my reach. I valued what was good in Mrs. Fairfax, and what was good in Adèle; but I (60)believed in the existence of other and more vivid kinds of goodness, and what I believed in I wished to behold.

Who blames me? Many, no doubt; and I shall be called discontented. I could not help it: the (65)restlessness was in my nature; it agitated me to pain sometimes. Then my sole relief was to walk along the corridor of the third storey, backwards and forwards, safe in the silence and solitude of the spot, and allow my mind's eye to (70)dwell on whatever bright visions rose before it—and, certainly, they were many and glowing; to let my heart be heaved by the exultant movement, which, while it swelled it in trouble, expanded it with life; and, best of all, to open my (75)inward ear to a tale that was never ended—a tale my imagination created, and narrated continuously; quickened with all of incident, life, fire, feeling, that I desired and had not in my actual existence.

(80)It is in vain to say human beings ought to be satisfied with tranquillity: they must have action; and they will make it if they cannot find it. Millions are condemned to a stiller doom than mine, and millions are in silent revolt against (85)their lot. Nobody knows how many rebellions besides political rebellions ferment in the masses of life which people earth. Women are supposed to be very calm generally: but women feel just as men feel; they need exercise (90)for their faculties, and a field for their efforts, as much as their brothers do; they suffer from too rigid a restraint, too absolute a stagnation, precisely as men would suffer; and it is narrow-minded in their more privileged (95)fellow-creatures to say that they ought to confine themselves to making puddings and knitting stockings, to playing on the piano and embroidering bags. It is thoughtless to condemn them, or laugh at them, if they seek to do more or (100)learn more than custom has pronounced necessary for their sex.

13. In the beginning of the passage, Jane describes Mrs. Fairfax as

   A. restrained and cold.

   B. rebellious and emotional.

   C. vivacious and cheerful.

   D. obedient and teachable.

   E. kind and even-tempered.

14. In the beginning of the fourth paragraph, Jane says:

   Who blames me? Many, no doubt; and I shall be called discontented. I could not help it: the restlessness was in my nature; it agitated me to pain sometimes.

   These lines show that Jane is

   A. confused about her feelings.

   B. angry because people don't understand her.

   C. realistic about how others may perceive her.

   D. worried that others may dislike her.

   E. guilty about her feelings towards Adèle.

15. When Jane says "Who blames me?", the literary device being used is called a(n)
    A. paradox
    B. understatement
    C. hyperbole
    D. rhetorical question
    E. simile

16. Which type of literary device is used in the following lines?

    Then my sole relief was to walk along the corridor of the third storey, backwards and forwards, safe in the silence and solitude of the spot, and allow my mind's eye to dwell on whatever bright visions rose before it—and, certainly, they were many and glowing...

    A. simile
    B. imagery
    C. pun
    D. allusion
    E. irony

17. The statement "millions are condemned to a stiller doom than mine, and millions are in silent revolt against their lot" (lines 83-85) implies that
    A. people are responsible their own success.
    B. revolts are inevitable in society.
    C. Jane realizes her life could be much worse.
    D. Jane feels guilty about her thoughts of escape.
    E. Jane is bored and dissatisfied with her life.

18. The word "stagnation" (line 93) is closest in meaning to which of the following words?
    A. confinement
    B. fascination
    C. decay
    D. placid
    E. monotony

19. When Jane refers to the "more privileged fellow-creatures" (lines 94–95), she is talking about
    A. children
    B. animals
    C. women
    D. men
    E. the upper-class

20. When discussing activities such as playing the piano and knitting stockings, Brontë is suggesting that
    A. men are not as skilled at these pursuits and consequently avoid them.
    B. women should only pursue one hobby and avoid trying to do too many things at once.
    C. women's activities should not be determined solely by the gender norms of the time.
    D. these activities help prevent boredom and unhappiness among women.
    E. women perform the most important work in a household.

21. Jane would most likely agree with which of the following statements?
    A. People are naturally inclined to seek out excitement in life.
    B. People should not complain about circumstances in their life.
    C. Men and women are more content when they have hobbies to pursue.
    D. Women and men do not experience emotions in the same way.
    E. Children are ungrateful towards the people who teach them.

22. All of the following words describe Jane's mood in this passage EXCEPT
    A. tranquil
    B. unsettled
    C. contemplative
    D. passionate
    E. apathetic

23. Overall, Jane is dissatisfied because

A. she is frustrated by Adèle's lack of progress.

B. she longs to have more excitement and vigor in her life.

C. she feels mistreated and neglected by her superiors.

D. she wants to find a husband.

E. she does not think she is a good governess.

24. Which of the following words does NOT reflect a theme of this passage?

A. egocentrism

B. gender relations

C. desire for freedom

D. restlessness

E. responsibility

Section II

24 Questions

Time – 25 Minutes

For each question in this section, select the best answer from the choices given and fill in the corresponding blank.

Each sentence below has one or two blanks, each blank indicating that something has been omitted. Beneath the sentence are five choices, labeled A through E. Choose the word or combination of words that, when placed in the sentence, *best* fits the sentence's meaning.

1. During a break in the _____ we sought _____ in a quiet corner.

A. bedlam… refuge

B. silence… rejuvenation

C. disorder… succor

D. din… refreshment

E. clamor… banishment

2. Because the soil seemed to _____ them a living, the settlers learned to make do in other ways.

A. begrudge   D. oblige

B. beguile   E. indulge

C. belabor

3. The atoll's immense lagoon is lined with mangrove trees, which make a _____ and breeding ground for several species of tropical birds.

A. canopy   D. chamber

B. steppe   E. shrine

C. sanctuary

4. If there are any _____ about getting an insect deemed a health hazard, you won't hear them in Florence County, South Carolina. Last year they saw most of their harvest lost to infestation.

A. quagmires   D. differentials

B. qualms   E. proclivities

C. pretenses

5. Cliffs of hard, gray _____ rose thousands of feet on either side as we trudged up the mountain.

   A.   steel
   B.   granite
   C.   grange
   D.   nuggets
   E.   cardboard

The next passages are followed by questions based on content. Questions following a pair of related passages may also ask how the passages relate to one another. Answer the questions on the basis of what is *stated* or *implied* in the passages as well as any introductory material provided.

Questions 6–9 are based on the following passages:

Passage 1

The North had many advantages in fighting the Civil War compared to the South. Besides a far greater manufacturing capability, the North had roughly seven (5)times the population as the South, giving them a much greater ability to assemble an army. The Union was also able to capitalize on a source of dedicated and eager recruits in the form of former slaves (10)who had escaped or migrated to the cities and farms of the northeast. Even slaves who did not flee the North could be of service to the United States and often provided the Northern Army with (15)valuable information on the troop movements and actions of the Confederates. The early Union strategy included a naval blockade against the South and a plan to invade Virginia in order to capture (20)the Confederate capital at Richmond.

Passage 2

The South was not without its own advantages, however. First, the South had many of the most talented leaders in the proper commands early in the war—men (25)like Robert E. Lee and Thomas "Stonewall" Jackson. Second, the vast majority of the war was fought on Southern soil. While this was some disadvantage in that Southerners suffered most of (30)the damage to their farms and homes, familiarity with the land gave the Confederates a better feel for how to conduct the war and how to evade the enemy. Finally, the South was able to use a much larger (35)proportion of its male population in military service, and thus was able to lessen the North's numeric advantage. These factors, despite the Confederacy's material disadvantages and lesser overall (40)population, made it possible for the South to achieve great success during the early years of the war.

6. The South's smaller population was likely a disadvantage *after the war* because

   A.   the South's ability to make weapons was hindered.
   B.   the South could not raise as large an army as the North for future wars.
   C.   too many of the Southern men migrated to the North.
   D.   the North's manufacturing ability hurt the South's economy.
   E.   not enough Southern men survived the war to help rebuild the South.

7. Which of the following best describes the relationship between the two passages?

   A.   The two passages offer complimentary evidence.

   B.   Passage 2 compares the ideas of Passage 1.

   C.   Passage 2 refutes the evidence supporting the assertions of Passage 1.

   D.   Passage 2 continues the claims and logic set forth in Passage 1.

   E.   Passage 1 offers support to the ideas of Passage 2.

8. Both passages are concerned with the

   A.   disadvantages of the North Army.

   B.   disadvantages of the Southern Army.

   C.   the dedicated army of soldiers on both sides.

   D.   manufacturing strength of the two sides.

   E.   various advantages and weaknesses of two armies in the Civil War.

9. According to the passage, what two factors likely contributed the most to the South not being able to win the war?

   A.   the mistakes made by their leaders and their lack of weaponry

   B.   the larger army and material superiority of the North

   C.   their knowledge of the land and their will to fight

   D.   the excellence of Northern leaders and its expansive railroad system

   E.   the lack of a solid manufacturing economy and a shortage of good leaders

Questions 10–18 are based on the following passage:

The United States government is known worldwide as a leader in managing the economic and political affairs of the nation and for advising its international (5)neighbors. To explain in detail is to use the example of how the federal government has worked out situations affecting trade of goods between the states and also abroad. In addition, its domestic policies (10)in relation to revenue generating are worth noting. Domestically, we trade goods that are manufactured or grown in the country between all the states with relatively little problem; but when we (15)ship those goods overseas, it becomes complicated. The process itself is called *exporting* and how well it works depends upon certain factors, such as the quantity of goods shipped, the type of goods, (20)where the goods are being shipped to, et cetera. The United States also takes in goods from other countries through a process called *importing*. The federal government monitors the nation's inventory as (25)well as its economic flow of goods shipped out or taken in through a system called *balance of trade*. It is important to be mindful of how many goods are exported versus how many are imported (30)because if imported goods are worth more in value than exported goods, a *trade deficit* results. A trade deficit can be harmful to various sectors of the nation's economy if it continues for a prolonged (35)period of time.

In negotiating agreements, policies, or treaties with other countries, it is important to have diplomatic recognition. This means it is not only (40)essential to be aware of cultural differences between various nations but to also be skillful at managing the relations between all of the different countries involved. Many factors are involved in (45)doing business with people of foreign lands, since all have different ideologies and practices. It requires patience and education to understand these differences and to make sound international trade (50)agreements.

Domestic policies also encompass a wide range of issues and matters from government revenue to the amendments within the Constitution. To begin with, **(55)**there are multiple sources of government revenue. One of the largest sources of money for the federal government is taxes on citizens. There are different taxation systems. One type is called a **(60)***proportional* tax. This means that the same percentage comes from every citizen, regardless of variation in income earned by each individual. A second type of tax is called the *progressive* tax. This **(65)**tax is based upon the amount of income an individual earns. The progressive tax system uses a sliding scale to determine how much a person pays. *Regressive* tax is a tax placed upon **(70)**products, materials, services, et cetera, and does not factor in the amount of income a person earns. An example of this type of tax is sales tax. In this example, people choose how much they pay by **(75)**making the decision to buy or not to buy items.

There are also specific types of tax the federal government collects from an individual's income. The main one is the **(80)**federal income tax, which currently uses the progressive tax system mentioned earlier. There is also FICA, which contributes to the federal social security system. Another way the federal government **(85)**receives taxes is by *tariffs*. In the past, the government taxed imported and exported goods (even between states), but now taxes imports exclusively.

Other sources of government revenue **(90)**would include generating money from fines, licenses, user fees and from a person borrowing money such as on a loan from a bank. Fines would include a penalty an individual would pay to the Internal **(95)**Revenue Service if federal income

taxes were underpaid or if a company violated Environmental Protection Agency regulations. Revenue that comes from borrowing passes from the lending rate the **(100)**government gives to banks for "borrowing" the money and then to the individuals borrowing the money from the banks. This rate passes from the government, to the banks and then to individuals, **(105)**in the form of an *interest rate*.

10. According to the passage, government tariffs would include
    A. items shipped from New York to Baltimore.
    B. items shipped from New Orleans to Tokyo.
    C. items brought in from Thailand.
    D. anything the United States manufactures.
    E. goods made by illegal immigrants.

11. The use of the word "complicated" in line 16 mostly likely means
    A. complex and technical.
    B. open to interpretation.
    C. hard to understand.
    D. not worth bothering about.
    E. inconvenient.

12. It can be inferred from the passage about the Environmental Protection Agency (line 97) that fines are paid by
    A. individuals who litter.
    B. banks that pollute the lending market.
    C. other nations who do business in the United States.
    D. people that cheat on their income taxes.
    E. private businesses that pollute illegally.

13. The word "exclusively" in line 88 most nearly means

    A.   harshly.

    B.   only.

    C.   without regard to right or wrong.

    D.   since the beginning of the nation.

    E.   until the tariff is repealed.

14. The author explains the different types of earning opportunities for governments in order to

    A.   argue how and why taxes are unfair to working people.

    B.   explain how the government exploits other nations.

    C.   show how the United States government gets money to run its programs.

    D.   show how different nations earn money.

    E.   argue why the United States is better than other countries.

15. In lines 54–83, the author explains different kinds of taxes by

    A.   defining each one and giving examples.

    B.   listing the definition and legal regulation.

    C.   naming each and explaining how it works.

    D.   providing the history of each tax.

    E.   arguing why each is unfair to working people.

16. The first paragraph of the passage serves to

    A.   explain why the United States is different than other nations.

    B.   claim the United States should do more for other nations.

    C.   introduce the reader to the complexities of international relations and revenue generation.

    D.   argue that taxes are wrong.

    E.   define some types of revenue sources for governments.

17. It can be inferred from the passage that international relations

    A.   often hinge on fair and balanced trade with other nations.

    B.   involve diplomacy, negotiation, and a strong military.

    C.   explain that unfair trade balances can lead to war.

    D.   are a chief source of income for the United States.

    E.   are based on low tariffs alone.

18. What is the best way to describe the organization of this passage?

    A.   cause-effect

    B.   contrasting ideas

    C.   problem-solution

    D.   order of importance

    E.   chronological order

Questions 19–24 are based on this passage:

The following passage, written in the 1990s, addresses efforts to equalize pay scales between men and women.

The history of wage theory began with St. Thomas Aquinas. His philosophy was that the wages of workers should provide them with a standard of living that (5)reflects their social standing. That is a perfect description of the second-class wages that women, as the perennial second-class citizens, have received and still receive.

(10)As early as the 1950s, women's groups organized and called attention to the issue of gender inequalities in pay. At this time, men held the top managerial positions in virtually every profession. (15)Women were often told that being a homemaker was the only or best option available for fulfillment in life. Women who chose to work, moreover, faced an uphill battle in trying to get jobs that went (20)beyond menial or clerical status. When women first tried to break into male-dominated fields in the workplace, such as the acting profession and teaching, they had to undergo a great deal of (25)discrimination and harassment and were often hired at rates less than those of men. In some cases, women came to completely fill an economic niche such as clerical positions. Once clerical positions (30)became almost exclusively women's work, and no man would touch them, women found that their wages never approached what men had earned as the majority in that position.

(35)In recent history, however, change has come at a more rapid pace. Women have entered the workforce in greater numbers. The number of women in the workforce has increased from 38 (40)percent in 1960 to nearly 60 percent in

1997. In particular, women have entered the white-collar professional jobs at increasingly higher rates. Because of higher attendance at universities and (45)colleges across the nation, the number of women professionals has rapidly increased. Women now enjoy full participation in the professions of law, medicine, and management. In some cases, more (50)women are enrolled in graduate programs than men!

Despite these great strides that have taken place in employment, there is a shrinking but still persistent difference (55)between what women make and what men make for the same job. As a whole, the upward mobility of women has led to an increase in women's pay rates. However, the salary difference still hovers (60)around 20 percent. The earnings of women in all ranks, in all professions, must be addressed.

A major symptom of the problem and a disability that women have carried (65)historically is embedded in the English language. When the position was "stewardess," wages were low; now, "flight attendants" make more. When the position was "waitress," wages were low; (70)now, "servers" make more. Notice, too, the war-like language used to describe the highest level of gender discrimination: "One obstacle to closing this gap is the breaking of the 'glass ceiling.'" The glass (75)ceiling, however, is a real barrier that women experience as they try to move into the upper echelons of the company environment. The upper levels, almost entirely dominated by men, tend to (80)promote other men to the highest positions in the company. This "Good Old Boys" system of upper management thwarts the earning potential of women. Because these positions pay several times (85)more annually than the lower positions, this phenomenon can explain some of the pay discrepancy.

Fresh solutions are needed to close the continuing gender gap. While there **(90)**has been some headway in women achieving the highest positions in major corporations, the changes are almost too small to consider. Possible strategies to address the glass ceiling include sending a **(95)**bill through Congress. This bill would require corporations to explain the reasons for their promotion decisions to a special board if the companies' policies are called into question by other employees. In **(100)**addition, women can start their own companies, becoming their own CEOs— starting at the top. Plans of action are needed and should be considered as soon as possible to address the wide gap in pay.

– Reprinted from <u>Equal Pay Rights: The Struggle Continues</u> by Jennifer Winters, published in New York by Goldwater Press, 1999

19. The word "niche" in line 28 most nearly means

- A. small office.
- B. specialized area.
- C. place in the economy.
- D. area reserved for men only.
- E. wide open job market.

20. According to the passage, the English language has changed in respect to the workplace, as now

- A. change has come at a more rapid pace in recent history.
- B. women's groups call attention to the issue of gender inequalities in pay.
- C. women have entered the workforce in greater numbers.
- D. jobs pay more when their titles do not indicate gender.
- E. positions held by men are diminishing.

21. The author's tone in paragraph 6 can best be described as

- A. unhappy and frustrated.
- B. disheartened and cynical.
- C. angry and grieved.
- D. hostile and distrusting.
- E. indignant and self-assured.

22. According to St. Thomas Aquinas, in lines 1–5, workers should receive

- A. a universal wage.
- B. a wage set by the government.
- C. a wage that reflects their place in society.
- D. wages determined by their bosses.
- E. a minimum hourly wage.

23. The first two sentences are characterized, respectively, by

- A. disclaimer and rebuttal.
- B. citation and definition.
- C. apology and confession.
- D. invocation and assertion.
- E. anecdote and humor.

24. As used in line 65, "embedded" most nearly means

- A. carved into rock.
- B. become a permanent part of traditional practice.
- C. sunken underground.
- D. only used for short periods.
- E. adapted into practice on a wait-and-see basis.

Section III

19 Questions

Time – 20 Minutes

> For each question in this section, select the best answer from the choices given and fill in the corresponding blank.
>
> Each sentence below has one or two blanks, each blank indicating that something has been omitted. Beneath the sentence are five choices, labeled A through E. Choose the word or combination of words that, when placed in the sentence, *best* fits the sentence's meaning.

1. Despite the ongoing _____ over his motives for running in the election and the aggressive smear campaigns against him, Fredrick _____ his opponent in a land-slide.

   A. deliberation... negated
   B. debate... defeated
   C. equivocation... compensated
   D. rivalry... succeeded
   E. contention... eclipsed

2. Although most people associate Arizona with a desert climate, the northern part of the state _____ with forests and has a(n) _____ cooler climate, with snow in the winter and relatively mild summers.

   A. is replete... inversely
   B. teems... exorbitantly
   C. fluctuates... inexplicably
   D. resides... assiduously
   E. abounds... appreciably

3. Due to their continuing _____ differences in artistic vision and _____ reviews from literary critics, the three writers decided not to put their names on the new book.

   A. collaboration on... optimistic
   B. pioneering... unprofessional
   C. quarrel over... derogatory
   D. temporal... dynamic
   E. compulsive... conservative

4. After _____ collecting fragments from the space shuttle *Columbia* explosion, investigators concluded the accident was caused by human error due to sleep deprivation.

   A. comprehensively
   B. tediously
   C. posthumously
   D. allegorically
   E. haphazardly

5. Although all foods contain a _____ amount of toxins, a healthy person with a varied diet is in little danger of becoming ill from consuming any one particular toxin in small quantities.

   A. radicalized   D. gregarious
   B. parasitic   E. tacit
   C. minute

6. Three times, rain and falling rock _____ their efforts to climb further up the slope.

- A. mitigated
- B. scourged
- C. eroded
- D. stooped
- E. thwarted

The next passages are followed by questions based on content. Questions following a pair of related passages may also ask how the passages relate to one another. Answer the questions below on the basis of what is *stated* or *implied* in the passages as well as any introductory material provided.

Questions 7–19 are based on these passages:

Passage 1 discusses the rise to power of Benito Mussolini, who led a fascist Italy to the edge of European conquest in the 1940s. The second passage discusses Adolf Hitler's political ascendance and policies.

Passage 1

After World War I, Benito Mussolini further developed a set of political ideas he called fascism. Mussolini dreamed of revitalizing an Italian empire, using as his **(5)**inspiration and guiding thought the imperial heritage of ancient Rome. He hoped to accomplish this by strict government controls and a strong military directed toward achieving a rigorous set of **(10)**nationalistic goals. Totalitarian by design, his Fascist Party opposed workers' strikes in the cities and peasants' strikes in the country and in the process gaining the support of those who feared the spread of **(15)**communism: conservative business leaders and landlords, the Roman Catholic Church, and the army.

By 1921–22, Italy's democratic constitutional monarchy government was in **(20)**crisis. Pouncing on the political confusion, Mussolini established himself as dictator, banning all political parties except for his own. He abolished labor unions, forbade strikes, and silenced **(25)**political opponents while preserving a capitalist economy and increased military power. As dictator of Italy from 1922 to 1945, Mussolini transformed the state into a militaristic and nationalist instrument of **(30)**conquest called expansionism by political scholara. *Fascist expansionism* was a policy implemented by Mussolini that encouraged aggressive maneuvers to overtake other nations. By way of **(35)**roundabout implementation, this desire to conquer led him to send military troops to fellow fascist Francisco Franco, who was then fighting the Spanish Civil War against an international army of **(40)**anti-fascist volunteers.

There are multiple factors that must combine for a total fascist regime to operate. There has to be oppression of the conquered citizens, a strong and mobile **(45)**military force, and a sustaining power which can use violence. Another facet to the requirements for fascism is called the *glorification of the state*. This concept is based on propaganda used by the **(50)**government in an attempt to rally support for its cause. This may be accomplished through national celebrations, elaborate parades, or even speeches given from those in power.

Passage 2

(55) Economic hardship followed Germany's humiliating defeat at the end of World War I. The democratic government established in 1919 failed to provide solutions to post-war conditions and **(60)**German society began to collapse. As the nation suffered through the Great Depression, armed gangs of fascists and communists roamed the streets forcing the government to use emergency measures. **(65)**The fascists, calling themselves Nazis, steadily gained support from a desperate, frightened people who believed they'd been cheated out of victory in WWI by incompetent government and **(70)**military leadership.

The Nazis' Führer, (or "father") Adolf Hitler, preached a message of racist fascism, claiming that the Aryan race (Caucasian people of non-Jewish descent) **(75)**was superior and deserved to conquer other nations through a policy of *genocide*: the extermination of a cultural or racial group of people. Hitler harbored prejudices towards other groups of **(80)**individuals such as Slavs, homosexuals, and Catholics, but saved his purest vitriol for the Jews. Hitler blamed Germany's economic struggles principally on Jews and on the Triple Entente nations **(85)**who had imposed harsh war reparations (money penalties) at the Treaty of Versailles, ending World War One but imposing humiliating restrictions on the German people and economy. Hitler's **(90)**message of national superiority and scapegoating attracted Germans who were reeling from economic and patriotic hardship.

In January 1933, the German **(95)**president responded to Hitler's strong popular support by appointing him Chancellor, or head of the government. In a series of political moves, Hitler dismantled all opposition to the Nazis and **(100)**established himself as dictator. Fulfilling his promise to rebuild Germany, Hitler violated the Treaty of Versailles by rejuvenating the military, creating a new

air force, and re-establishing the draft. The **(105)**Gestapo (secret police) helped Hitler suppress dissenters, putting all aspects of society under Nazi control.

Under Hitler, Germany inflicted dreadful atrocities on the Jewish people **(110)**during World War II. Hitler and his henchmen rounded up all the Jews in Germany and had them shipped to concentration camps, where six million of them were gassed or shot to death. The carnage **(115)**continued until 1945, when Allied incursions into Germany liberated the camps and drove Hitler to suicide inside his heavily-fortified bunker.

7. In line 42, "regime" most closely means a

    A. form of government.
    B. political party.
    C. social class.
    D. military build-up.
    E. philosophical idea.

8. Both Mussolini and Hitler believed in

    A. reducing the military and increasing government controls.
    B. isolationism and financial independence.
    C. revamping the economy through government regulation.
    D. a strong military and a complete devotion to country.
    E. reverting to an agrarian economy.

9. The passages imply that Mussolini and Hitler were most alike in that they

   A. were both interested in the common good.

   B. tried to move their nations toward expansion.

   C. both secretly spread propaganda about their political goals.

   D. worked to provide a better place for their countrymen.

   E. believed they were divinely inspired.

10. In Passage 1, the phrase "glorification of the state" most closely means

   A. to fear outsiders who are not fascists.

   B. to honor the friendly nations you come in contact with.

   C. to show patriotism when interacting with immigrants.

   D. to revile countries who do not share your country's ideals.

   E. to put all energies into honoring and respecting one's own government.

11. The first two paragraphs of each passage both present

   A. scientific theories

   B. historical summaries

   C. a list of sources

   D. speculatory evidence

   E. introductory asides

12. The politics of both Mussolini and Hitler mainly relied on

   A. power through violence and suppression of the citizenry.

   B. a strong central government with vast voting rights.

   C. the support of the majority party.

   D. great celebrations and clever propaganda.

   E. the weakness of the surrounding nations.

13. The term "genocide" in context with these two leaders most closely means

   A. the deportation of Jews and radicals.

   B. the total extermination of political and ethnic opponents.

   C. the mass execution of government officials.

   D. the elimination of the elderly.

   E. the banishment of citizens who opposed their views.

14. According to the passages, both Mussolini and Hitler came to power

   A. during harsh economic times in their countries.

   B. just after World War II.

   C. after a previous leader had died.

   D. with few promises of great things for their countries.

   E. promising to attack the nations of the Triple Entente.

15. Both passages imply that the citizens of Italy and Germany both

   A. were concerned with the path their country was taking.

   B. were completely devoted to their leader.

   C. rallied behind their leader rather than risk death or banishment.

   D. felt their old leaders knew what was best for them.

   E. hated their leader and his political maneuverings.

16. According to the passages, dictators and fascists do all of the following EXCEPT

   A. use their words and speeches to spread their message.

   B. plot to take over countries with weak militaries.

   C. prey on the ignorance of the citizenry.

   D. possess a fear or hatred of people different from themselves.

   E. work through proper channels to gain power.

17. The term "atrocities" in line 109 most nearly means
    A. horrible retaliation for their crimes.
    B. terrible destruction of homes and towns by the Nazi party.
    C. punishment of dissenters by the Gestapo.
    D. reduction of goods and services to the people.
    E. appalling acts of cruelty inflicted by force.

18. The tone of the author in both passages is one of
    A. objectivity.
    B. caution.
    C. outrage.
    D. resentment.
    E. tolerance.

19. In line 109, "dreadful" most nearly means
    A. insignificant.
    B. horrible.
    C. unprecedented.
    D. carefully planned.
    E. monumental.

SAT Reading Preparation
Practice Test 2

Section I
24 Questions
Time – 25 minutes

Directions: For each question in this section, select the best answer from among the given choices.

Each sentence below has one or two blanks, each blank indicating that something has been omitted. Beneath the sentence are five choices, labeled A through E. Choose the word or combination of words that, when placed in the sentence, *best* fits the sentence's meaning.

Example: Bob worried it was only a matter of time before Katie_____; she'd been enthusiastic about the plan yesterday, but he expected her to feel differently once she gave the idea serious _____.

A. wavered… decision
B. obliged… hesitation
C. demurred… consideration
D. argued… rethinking
E. exited… reconciliation

The correct answer is *C*.

1. In 1865, the Hawaiian government admitted that it faced a strange and terrible new disease of leprosy, an epidemic of the most _____ sort.

   A. viscous   D. violable
   B. vigilant   E. vitreous
   C. virulent

2. Patrick raised himself from the age of ten, a loner who took a certain _____ pride in the _____ path such a life required.

   A. deliberate… prosaic
   B. righteous… vigilant
   C. gleeful… surreal
   D. arrogant… solitary
   E. insolent… synthetic

3. He had an alert, _____ look, like a black cat that could smell a nest of baby mice.

   A. princely   D. foreboding
   B. desolate   E. ravenous
   C. morose

4. Squeezing past clusters of stray dogs and naked children, I peered into _____ small houses where families of twelve or more people lived.

   A. imposingly   D. inadvertently
   B. impossibly   E. inconsistently
   C. impressively

5. Writing papers in college forced me to become _____ on the keyboard.

   A. impotent   D. flamboyant
   B. disposable   E. dynamic
   C. proficient

The passages below are followed by questions based on content. Questions following a pair of related passages may also ask how the passages relate to one another. Answer the questions below on the basis of what is *stated* or *implied* in the passages as well as any introductory material provided.

Questions 6–7 are based on this passage:

During the 1890s, a social and political movement called Progressivism developed in response to growing corruption in politics and business. Progressives (5)championed the cause of making government more accountable to the people and less beholden to business and industry. They fought to bring down big city bosses who had gained enormous wealth (10)and influence through bribery and corruption. Such corruption hurt the poor and immigrants the most because they could least afford it. One of the most infamous big city bosses, William Tweed,

(15)stole over 100 million dollars from the treasury of New York City.

6. What does the author mean by the phrase "championed the cause" of making government more accountable (line 5–7)?

   A. The government listened to the Progressives.
   B. The Progressives were leaders in the government.
   C. The Progressive party ruled New York.
   D. Corruption ran through the Progressive party.
   E. The Progressives deeply believed in this idea.

7. The theme of the passage is more

   A.   informative than persuasive.

   B.   inspirational than informative.

   C.   passionate than educational.

   D.   inspirational than expository.

   E.   persuasive than informative.

Questions 8–9 are based on this passage:

     In the unmistakable silence of dawn, before the sun rose and showered the landscape, I spied through the small opening of my tent the beauty of the morning and **(5)**dreamed how lucky I was to be here in one of the last strongholds of the African elephant. Then, across the hills of the African Game Reserve, a gunshot rang out and shattered all dreams. A terrible **(10)**stillness followed; then two, three, four shots followed and tore at my soul. In the distance, a helpless, wounded elephant limped away from the herd and hobbled into the heavy brush.

8. What is the narrator implying by referring to the place as "one of the last strongholds of the African elephant"?

   A.   This is an area where the elephants rule the other animals.

   B.   This is one place on Earth where elephants are still in abundance.

   C.   This area is off-limits to people.

   D.   The area is too wild for other animals.

   E.   The area is isolated and too desolate for humans.

9. The author's tone in the final sentence might best be described as

   A.   distrusting and suspicious.

   B.   angry and vengeful.

   C.   sad and sympathetic.

   D.   frustrated and disgusted.

   E.   encouraged and motivated.

The next passages are followed by questions based on content. Questions following a pair of related passages may also ask how the passages relate to one another. Answer the questions below on the basis of what is stated or implied in the passages as well as any introductory material provided.

Questions 10–17 are based on this passage:

The following is adapted from a 1999 Atlanta Journal-Constitution *article about immigration and naturalization (the process of becoming an American citizen). It focuses on the immigrants' perspective of the process of gaining American citizenship.*

     There were no doubts or second guesses. Salahuddin Jamil knew he wanted to be an American. "I had experience in Europe and America and my **(5)**home, a third world country," said Jamil, a Bangladesh native. "I have seen three sides, and there is no greater country than the USA."

     Each year, Congress decides how **(10)**many immigrants may enter America, and the number permitted has risen steadily. So has the rate of assimilation. A recent Census data report by the National Immigration Forum indicates that more **(15)**than two-thirds of U.S. immigrants speak English fluently within 10 years. It is largely this group that accounts for the increase in applicants to the Immigration and Naturalization Service seeking to **(20)**become American citizens.

     But it takes more than desire. The naturalization process is lengthy—taking as long as two years between the application and the citizenship oath. It includes **(25)**background checks, fingerprinting and tests—written and oral—with questions about history and politics.

Oksana Gerasimenko, a 31-year-old Ukrainian refugee, was among thousands **(30)**who took the oath in 1999. "The U.S. has always been a country of freedom, not England, not Japan or anywhere else," said Gerasimenko. "That's what I thought as I was growing up. I got that from the **(35)**movies and the books."

When Gerasimenko moved to Atlanta, she knew of about two dozen Russians in her area. But she's noticed that the population has increased lately to **(40)**almost 30,000. "Now, I hear Russian [spoken] in the grocery store, and anywhere I go," she said.

Gerasimenko's husband decided the couple would move to Atlanta in 1991 **(45)**because he felt the Olympics would create business opportunities. He now owns his own construction company and is among the thousands waiting to take the Oath of Allegiance.

(50) Jamil, 41, bought his first restaurant two years after becoming a citizen. He worked as a cook in an Indian restaurant and saved the bulk of his earnings. Then he made an agreement with a soon-**(55)**to-be-retiring couple that if he successfully ran their delicatessen, he could buy it from them at a bargain.

He now owns a successful sandwich shop in downtown Atlanta across the **(60)**street from the Immigration and Naturalization Service offices.

"John Kennedy's Peace Corps gave me respect for the USA," said Jamil. "Then I read about Martin Luther King, **(65)**and that is why I had to come here [to Atlanta]. We can eat together and stand together and work together because of him."

Jamil speaks proudly of the franchises **(70)**he has owned and sold, and the addition of hand-dipped ice cream to his store. He becomes passionate and forceful when he talks about the homeless drunk he hired and sent to a rehabilitation center.

(75)"We must do for the weaker person. All they need is love," he preaches with a clenched fist. "No one here is better than anyone else." It's part of the reason Jamil and several of his countrymen **(80)**started the Bangladesh Association, of which he is now a commissioner. The organization works toward civic and social goals.

As Gerasimenko waited in line to **(85)**relinquish her green card and sign her citizen certificate, she said she was nervous.

"For the test, you can prepare," she said. "This you can't."

(90) Holding the flag just beneath the oath she would soon repeat, Gerasimenko looked solemn as a recording of the Star-Spangled Banner played overhead. She stood between a woman from the Ukraine **(95)**and a man from Vietnam and repeated the Oath of Allegiance. Her vow to remain true to America was easy to make, she said.

"I didn't have any place where I was a **(100)**citizen," Gerasimenko said. "So this was not hard."

10. As used in line 12, "assimilation" can be inferred to mean

   A.   adopting the customs and traditions of a foreign place.

   B.   converting into sound.

   C.   learning to speak a language.

   D.   the rate of immigration.

   E.   how many people the government lets immigrate.

11. All of the following are facts taken from the passage EXCEPT

   A.   immigrants don't work as hard as American citizens.

   B.   more immigrants want to become U.S. citizens.

   C.   the rate of immigration to America grows every year.

   D.   becoming an American citizen is a complicated process.

   E.   Congress raises the number of immigrants each year.

12. The main idea of this passage can best be expressed as

   A.   the United States is a country of freedom.

   B.   immigrants really enjoy all of their experiences in the United States.

   C.   immigrants are becoming responsible citizens in the United States.

   D.   Kosovo refugees are making new homes in the United States.

   E.   it is important for immigrants to become successful in their new country.

13. The description of the ceremony in lines 90–96 serves to illustrate

   A.   the government's apathy about immigration.

   B.   the ethnic diversity of those wanting to become Americans.

   C.   why more people don't take the Oath of Allegiance.

   D.   why Gerasimenko wants to take the Oath of Allegiance.

   E.   that immigration isn't a certain path to financial security.

14. In line 16, "fluently" most nearly means

   A.   with great skill.

   B.   with great difficulty.

   C.   only with others of the speaker's own country of origin.

   D.   only to family members.

   E.   only while entering the United States.

15. The story of how Jamil came to own a delicatessen in Atlanta serves to

   A.   verify his claims about life in America.

   B.   act as a warning to other immigrants.

   C.   show how Americans reject immigrants' best efforts.

   D.   explain that Atlanta is a good city for immigrants.

   E.   dramatize a successful immigrant experience.

16. According to the passage, Jamil was inspired to come to the United States after

   A.   fleeing a war in his own country.

   B.   growing dissatisfied with life in Europe.

   C.   learning about the Olympics.

   D.   observing the Peace Corps and learning about Martin Luther King.

   E.   learning that a retired couple needed his help.

17. According to the passage, why did Gerasim-enko's family come to Atlanta?

    A. The Olympics offered a business opportunity.

    B. It was the cheapest place to live they could find.

    C. They had family already there.

    D. The Immigration and Naturalization Service assigned them there.

    E. They wanted to own a delicatessen.

Questions 18–24 are based on this passage:

Excerpt from *Anna Karenina*, by Leo Tolstoy

Vronsky had not even tried to sleep all that night. He sat in his armchair, looking straight before him or scanning the people who got in and out. If he had indeed on previous occasions struck and (5)impressed people who did not know him by his air of unhesitating composure, he seemed now more haughty and self-possessed than ever. He looked at people as if they were things. A nervous young man, a clerk in a law court, sitting (10)opposite him, hated him for that look. The young man asked him for a light, and entered into conversation with him, and even pushed against him, to make him feel that he was not a thing, but a person. But Vronsky gazed at him (15)exactly as he did at the lamp, and the young man made a wry face, feeling that he was losing his self-possession under the oppression of this refusal to recognize him as a person.

Vronsky saw nothing and no one. He felt himself (20)a king, not because he believed that he had made an impression on Anna—he did not yet believe that,—but because the impression she had made on him gave him happiness and pride.

What would come of it all he did not know, he (25)did not even think. He felt that all his forces, hitherto dissipated, wasted, were centered on one thing, and bent with fearful energy on one blissful goal. And he was happy at it. He knew only that he had told her the truth, that he had (30)come where she was, that all the happiness of his life, the only meaning in life for him, now lay in seeing and hearing her. And when he got out of the carriage at Bologova to get some seltzer water, and caught sight of Anna, (35)involuntarily his first word had told her just what he thought. And he was glad he had told her it, that she knew it now and was thinking of it. He did not sleep all night. When he was back in the carriage, he kept unceasingly going over (40)every position in which he had seen her, every word she had uttered, and before his fancy, making his heart faint with emotion, floated pictures of a possible future.

When he got out of the train at Petersburg, he felt (45)after his sleepless night as keen and fresh as after a cold bath. He paused near his compartment, waiting for her to get out. "Once more," he said to himself, smiling unconsciously, "once more I shall see her walk, (50)her face; she will say something, turn her head, glance, smile, maybe." But before he caught sight of her, he saw her husband, whom the station-master was deferentially escorting through the crowd. "Ah, yes! The husband." (55)Only now for the first time did Vronsky realize clearly the fact that there was a person attached to her, a husband. He knew that she had a husband, but had hardly believed in his existence, and only now fully believed in him, (60)with his head and shoulders, and his legs clad in black trousers; especially when he saw this husband calmly take her arm with a sense of property.

Seeing Alexey Alexandrovitch with his (65)Petersburg face and severely self-confident figure, in his round hat, with his rather prominent spine, he believed in him, and was aware of a disagreeable sensation, such as a man might feel tortured by thirst, who, on reaching a spring, (70)should find a dog, a sheep, or a pig, who has drunk of it and muddied the water. Alexey Alexandrovitch's manner of walking, with a swing of the hips and flat feet, particularly annoyed Vronsky. He could recognize in no one (75)but himself an indubitable right to love her. But she was still the same, and the sight of her affected him the same way, physically reviving him, stirring him, and filling his soul with rapture. He told his German valet, who ran up to (80)him from the second class, to take his things and go on, and he himself went up to her. He saw the first meeting between the husband and wife, and noted with a lover's insight the signs of slight reserve with which she spoke to her (85)husband. "No, she does not love him and cannot love him," he decided to himself.

18. Vronsky looks at people "as if they were things" (line 8) because

- A. he is consumed with thoughts of Anna.
- B. he feels that he is superior to them.
- C. he does not like being in crowds.
- D. he is tired and in a daze from his travels.
- E. he does not like talking to strangers.

19. What is Vronsky's "blissful goal" (line 28)?

- A. to be in Anna's presence and spend time with her
- B. to tell Alexey Alexandrovitch about his feelings for Anna
- C. to finally see what Anna's husband looks like
- D. to be invited to Anna's home
- E. to prove that he loves Anna

20. Which literary device is used in the following sentence?

> *When he got out of the train at Petersburg, he felt after his sleepless night as keen and fresh as after a cold bath.*

- A. allusion
- B. symbol
- C. analogy
- D. simile
- E. understatement

21. Based on lines 52 to 54, the reader can infer that Anna's husband is

- A. eager to greet his wife.
- B. a worker at the train station.
- C. nervous in large crowds.
- D. lost in the train station.
- E. a person of importance.

22. When does Vronsky conclude that Anna does not love her husband?

- A. when he sees Alexey Alexandrovitch for the first time
- B. when he speaks to Anna at Bologova
- C. when Anna tells Vronsky that she is unhappy
- D. when he sees how Anna interacts with her husband
- E. when he sees Alexey Alexandrovitch take Anna's arm

23. Vronsky's attitude towards Anna's husband is BEST described as _____.

- A. rueful
- B. disdainful
- C. admiring
- D. stolid
- E. covetous

24. The word "indubitable" (line 75) is closest in meaning to which of the following words?

- A. inconclusive
- B. controversial
- C. undeniable
- D. necessary
- E. debatable

Section II

24 Questions

Time – 25 Minutes

For each question in this section, select the best answer from the choices given and fill in the corresponding blank.

Each sentence below has one or two blanks, each blank indicating that something has been omitted. Beneath the sentence are five choices, labeled A through E. Choose the word or combination of words that, when placed in the sentence, *best* fits the sentence's meaning.

---

1. Caesar paid no attention to _____ standards of dress, ignoring accepted male conventions and even human decencies.

   A. admirable
   B. historical
   C. popular
   D. fashionable
   E. traditional

2. Since Professor Lindy's testimony relied on _____ sources, the court ruled it as _____ and dismissed the case.

   A. clinical… irrelevant
   B. reliable… ludicrous
   C. disparaging… ignorance
   D. idealist… implausible
   E. ambiguous… insubstantial

3. During the early years of filmmaking, D.W. Griffith's knowledge of the _____ of film structure and the methods of storytelling was unusually _____ for its time, and pioneered techniques still used today.

   A. conservation… perverse
   B. capacity… mundane
   C. fundamentals… sophisticated
   D. diversity… intensive
   E. attributes… conventional

4. Folklore—both oral and written—_____ in England, from the legends of King Arthur and Robin Hood to more _____ myths such as the Beast of Bodmin Boor.

   A. flourishes… contemporary
   B. propagates… incredulous
   C. seethes… credulous
   D. quarreled… unforeseen
   E. debated… profitable

5. The _____ old man walked down the street to the house where he grew up, to _____ old memories.

   A. haggard… neglect
   B. decrepit… extricate
   C. depraved… obliterate
   D. melancholy… reminisce over
   E. weary… enlighten

6. As there are only approximately 25 to 50 remaining panthers in the swamps of Florida, there has been a(n) _____ effort to save the _____ population.

   A. conceited… fractioned
   B. disorganized… forgotten
   C. earnest… engrossed
   D. engaged… increasing
   E. widespread… dwindling

7. Feeling _____ by the long lecture, Mark raised his hand to ask his professor to _____ some of the topics that were unclear.

    A. irritated... reiterate
    B. overwhelmed... contemplate
    C. invigorated... dissipate
    D. befuddled... clarify
    E. dismayed... alleviate

8. Based on _____ and genetic findings, most researchers agree Native Americans are descendants of people who _____ from northern Asia across the Bering Strait into Alaska.

    A. anthropological... migrated
    B. scientific... heralded
    C. definitive... dislocated
    D. metaphysical... transcended
    E. epistemic... integrated

The passages below are followed by questions based on content. Questions following a pair of related passages may also ask how the passages relate to one another. Answer the questions below on the basis of what is *stated* or *implied* in the passages as well as any introductory material provided.

Questions 9–12 are based on the following passages:

Passage 1

Physical processes can have an influence on how the society of a region is developed. Different societies have different demographics or characteristics: size, (5)growth patterns, ages, income, health statistics, etc. For instance, if a region has excellent soil and other favorable conditions for growing crops, a large population of farmers might migrate to that area. The (10)physical elements are already in place, but it takes the abilities and skills of people to use the land to its fullest potential. This situation lends itself to what is considered a *settlement pattern*. People, (15)perhaps from other areas, learn of the success of growing crops in a particular region and internally migrate to that place within their own country. This differs from the type of migration that occurred in (20)the late 1800s and early 1900s, when there was a large influx of individuals who immigrated into the United States from Europe. In present times, immigration is still a factor in the United States, with the (25)greatest migration coming generally from the Latin American regions of the world.

Passage 2

Internal migration also occurs when people move into an urban area because of (30)job opportunities or industries present there. This type of migration into a city might occur particularly when there is a high unemployment rate and a decreased standard of living in another area. (35)Circumstances often motivate people to relocate to a different area hoping for a better living situation or a better job. A high population density develops due to population growth as more people move (40)into that urban region, and eventually the result is *urban sprawl*: the overflow of a city's high population spilling over into surrounding areas without a plan or structure. The rapid new construction includes (45)homes, apartments, schools, and shopping centers, causing road systems and residential areas to be poorly developed. Suburbs have been created in an attempt to get people to spread out in an orderly

(50)fashion around the urban area instead of just within it.

9. The words "migrate" in Passage 1 and "urban sprawl" in Passage 2 both indicate

   A. that Americans left the cities to find a better life in the country.

   B. that Americans moved as economic and cultural opportunities demanded.

   C. the need for registering people when they move to a new area.

   D. that Americans move whenever they feel like it.

   E. the extent to which Americans moved around in the 19th century.

10. The use of italics when describing a *settlement pattern* in line 14 is intended to

   A. set aside a technical term for special attention.

   B. show a phrase that doesn't belong in the passage.

   C. reflect the author's fascination with technical terms.

   D. show disapproval for overtly complicated language.

   E. reflect popular tastes.

11. In the context of Passage 2, the phrase "an orderly fashion" in lines 49–50 is intended to

   A. show how people want to behave.

   B. act as a cry for help.

   C. contrast the chaotic infrastructure of urban cities.

   D. complain about people moving where their neighbors do.

   E. comparison to 19th century rural migration.

12. Which of the following best describes the relationship between the two passages?

   A. Passage 1 offers support to the ideas of Passage 2.

   B. Passage 2 criticizes the ideas of Passage 1.

   C. Passage 2 refutes the evidence supporting the assertions of Passage 1.

   D. Passage 2 continues the claims and logic set forth in Passage 1.

   E. The two passages offer nearly identical evidence.

Questions 13–24 are based on the following passages:

Passage 1 deals with events leading up to the outbreak of the Civil War; Passage 2 relates how the secessionist crisis of 1861 played out in Maryland, a state that was for decades previously identified as a "No Man's Land" between the North and South. As a war between the states became inevitable, Maryland, a slave state, found itself literally split between the two sides.

Passage 1

By the beginning of the 1860s, the secessionist and abolitionist crises throughout the states and territories had come to a boiling point. A number of (5)causes urged voices in the South towards secession, but at their heart was the issue of slavery. Despite his assertions to the contrary, leaders in the Southern states believed Abraham Lincoln would (10)challenge the two-century old practice, which would mean a crippling loss of cheap (albeit unethically-gained) labor. For Lincoln, maintaining the union of states was more important than any other (15)concern, including his personal dislike of the institution of slavery. The Southern states were also angered by the fact that Northern states did not always comply with the Fugitive Slave Clause of the US (20)Constitution, which promised that runaway slaves would be returned to their owners and were not free simply because they moved to a free state. The *Dred Scott v Sanford* decision, in which the Supreme **(25)**Court stated that former slaves in free states did not have legal standing because they were not citizens, dealt a powerful blow to abolitionists but did not end the controversy. Northerners were unhappy **(30)**with the decision because it overturned the "free-soil movement" that attempted to build a slavery free land in the West. Other issues played a role as well. Northerners wanted tariffs on **(35)** manufactured goods to protect their industries, but Southerners opposed tariffs because they wanted cheaper manufactured goods and did not want to endanger the lucrative trade relations they had with **(40)**Britain.

As tensions rose on both sides of the Mason-Dixon line, the country armed itself and braced for what almost everyone understood to be inevitable. On December **(45)**20, 1860, South Carolina decided to secede from the Union. Six other states followed suit by February 1861. Four more would withdraw from the Union when the war began at Bull Run, Virginia **(50)**on July 21, 1861. This would bring the total number of secessionist states to eleven, enough to outweigh the Union in size if not population and industrial development; enough to become a credible **(55)**nation in its own right if not checked, one that would almost certainly side against a reduced United States and with its trade-hungry European rivals.

Passage 2

As the battle lines were drawn, **(60)**Maryland was split between the North and the South. Maryland was a slave state, but did not rely on plantation agriculture to nearly the degree the Deep South did.

Evidence taken from the memoirs of **(65)**Maryland slaves, most notably the great abolitionist and orator Frederick Douglass, suggests that, compared to their brethren farther south, slaves in relatively industrialized Maryland were treated more **(70)**humanely and given educations and comforts uncommon among slaves in the Cotton Belt of the Deep South. Nevertheless, Maryland bore the weight of both sides of the crisis: owning slaves and **(75)**wanting to abolish slavery once and for all. Economically, Maryland's wealth was hinged upon its port city, Baltimore; the state was beholden to the industrial centers of the north—most notably **(80)**Pennsylvania, New York, and Massachusetts—for export of goods, and trembled before the possibility of separation from its northern client-states. Continued slavery and secession would mean losing **(85)**the markets of those states' cities, devastating its economy.

Four slave states remained on the side of the Union (Missouri, Kentucky, Delaware, and Maryland), but Southern **(90)**sympathizers were common in these states and routinely pressured their governments for secession. To the Union, the secession of Maryland represented a threat to Union border security. If Maryland **(95)**joined the Confederacy, Washington, DC, would find itself surrounded by Confederate territory. Concerned that Confederate sympathizers might succeed in swaying Maryland into the Confederate **(100)**camp, President Lincoln declared martial law in Maryland and suspended the right of *habeas corpus*, which guarantees a person cannot be imprisoned without being brought before a judge. The **(105)**president then jailed the strongest supporters of the Confederacy. As a result, Maryland backed down and its legislature voted to remain in the Union. The suspen-

sion would not be lifted until the end of
(110)the Civil War, four years later.

13. In line 16, "institution" most nearly means
    A. formal place of learning.
    B. mental asylum.
    C. correctional facility.
    D. long-standing practice.
    E. society.

14. The author of Passage 1 indicates that the
    end of the "free soil movement" (line 31)
    and tariffs (line 34) were
    A. reasons the South wanted to secede
       from the North.
    B. important reasons for Europe to boycott
       the South.
    C. reasons the North wanted to avoid a
       war.
    D. poor reasons to demand secession.
    E. reasons the North wanted a war with
       the South.

15. The term "tensions" in line 41 refers to the
    A. feeling of unease felt by one side of the
       secessionist debate.
    B. heated disagreements between North
       and South.
    C. strain to fit everyone in a limited land
       space.
    D. potential consequences of secession.
    E. means to secede peacefully.

16. The author of Passage 1 cites the Dred Scott
    Decision in lines 23–24 in order to
    A. describe a particular event in the
       months leading to the war.
    B. show how laws about slaves were
       already in place.
    C. demonstrate how the South ignored
       laws passed in the North.
    D. show the effects of the abolitionist
       cause.
    E. argue for more laws that enforce ant-
       slavery opinions.

17. The first paragraph of Passage 2 presents
    a(n)
    A. overview of conditions in Maryland.
    B. list of reasons for Maryland to secede.
    C. list of sources.
    D. introductory aside.
    E. scientific theory.

18. In Passage 2, the phrase "relatively industri-
    alized" (lines 68–69) indicates that
    A. there were few industries in Maryland.
    B. there were more industries in the South
       than Maryland.
    C. the industries of North and South were
       related.
    D. Maryland was more industrialized than
       the Southern states.
    E. industry was built up on both sides of
       the country.

19. The phrase "hinged upon… Baltimore,"
    within the context of Passage 2, indicates
    that
    A. Maryland's economy depended on the
       prosperity of Baltimore.
    B. Baltimore was the only entryway for
       goods into the South.
    C. the North would occupy Baltimore if
       war broke out.
    D. the South wanted to invade Baltimore.
    E. Baltimore wanted slaves, but Mary-
       land did not.

20. The attitudes towards secession and aboli-
    tionism in both passages can be described as
    A. uninterested and uncaring.
    B. enthused and involved.
    C. open-mined and hopeful.
    D. skeptical and morose.
    E. dispassionate and interested.

21. The author of Passage 1 would be most likely to argue that the author of Passage 2

   A. did not consider that Maryland's secession would also harm the North.

   B. the fact that almost all Marylanders wanted to secede.

   C. failed to remember Maryland's pre-colonial history.

   D. improperly researched slave conditions in the South.

   E. didn't want to rely purely on speculation.

22. In lines 99–100, "the Confederate camp" is understood to mean

   A. all the states and people in favor of secession.

   B. anyone outside Maryland.

   C. everyone in the South.

   D. only those people in Maryland who wanted slavery.

   E. where Confederate leaders slept.

23. The attitude of the author of Passage 2 towards the people of Maryland is largely

   A. polite and compassionate.

   B. snide and critical.

   C. openly hostile.

   D. vaguely affectionate.

   E. scholarly and detached.

24. The authors of both passages might likely agree that

   A. Abraham Lincoln should not have declared martial law.

   B. the Civil War could have easily been avoided.

   C. slavery in the North was better than in the South.

   D. both the North and South stood to lose from secession.

   E. the Civil War came about almost overnight.

Section III

19 Questions

Time – 20 Minutes

For each question in this section, select the best answer from the choices given and fill in the corresponding blank.

Each sentence below has one or two blanks, each blank indicating that something has been omitted. Beneath the sentence are five choices, labeled A through E. Choose the word or combination of words that, when placed in the sentence, *best* fits the sentence's meaning.

---

1. Practically all important business decisions have to be _____ and approved in triplicate, _____ mounds of paperwork in the central office.

   A. organized… eliminating
   B. formulated… modifying
   C. examined… removing
   D. surveyed… originating
   E. reviewed… generating

2. Studies on attention have in the past focused on the extent to which adults can control whether their attention wanders by ignoring _____ information.

   A. essential   D. digressional
   B. obsolescent   E. pertinent
   C. irrelevant

3. With scant reserves of minerals and metals, the Swiss learned early in their history to apply a maximum amount of _____ to a _____ of raw materials.

   A. ingenuity… minimum
   B. brainpower… miniscule
   C. laziness… shortage
   D. ingenuousness… abundance
   E. ingenious… deficiency

4. When Carrie started junior high, she left a(n) _____, self-contained sixth grade classroom for a much larger _____ school, causing her anxiety and loneliness.

   A. intense… uncertain
   B. intimate… impersonal
   C. comfortable… elitist
   D. orderly… impressive
   E. transitory… congenial

5. The writer _____ three chapters of his book to satisfy editors who _____ its 1,000-page length.

   A. expanded…. deprecated
   B. annihilated… appreciated
   C. eliminated… esteemed
   D. condensed… disparaged
   E. decimated… respected

6. My grandma, a _____ woman barely five feet tall, and my grandpa, an imposing, _____ man who was once a heavyweight boxer, raised me from the age of two.

   A. statuesque… noble
   B. graceful… gargantuan
   C. miniscule… cadaverous
   D. miniature… enormous
   E. diminutive… burly

Questions 7–19 are based on this passage:

Where is the safest place for a mother to give birth to her baby? You may think a hospital, but the facts show that the mother's own home is just as safe—if not **(5)**safer—when a trained midwife attends the birth. This may seem like a strange idea, but for millennia women gave birth at home; only in recent centuries have they come to natal term in **(10)**hospitals. Age-old wisdom and modern science are coming together to show that for a woman with a healthy pregnancy, her own home is the safest birthplace because she is in a familiar **(15)**environment, surrounded by loved ones and free from standardized hospital policies.

Pregnant women must feel safe and comfortable or they will have interrupted **(20)**labor. This fact is recognized in the animal world but often neglected in regard to human mothers. For example, when a doe feels labor coming on, she seeks out a secure and protected place to give birth. If **(25)**she detects a predator approaching, her contractions will stop, so that she can run away and find another safe spot. Once settled in, her labor will resume. In a similar way, many women progress well in **(30)**their labor at home, but when they arrive at the hospital their labor slows down. Sometimes, the hospital even sends the woman home, where her contractions will resume normal progression. The **(35)**disruption and anxiety of the trip to the hospital can cause a woman's labor to slow or halt. If she remains in the safety and comfort of her home throughout labor

and delivery, her birth experience will **(40)**probably follow a more natural and rhythmic pattern.

A more important factor in the woman's feeling of safety and comfort is the presence of loving and supportive **(45)**friends and family. This may seem like a nice extra that has little biological effect on the birthing process, but there are significant differences between births of women with and without help. The **(50)**comforting presence of a friend or family member leads to diminished desire or need for anesthetic drugs and fewer surgical procedures known in medical terminology as "Cesarean" sections. Many **(55)**hospitals still place limitations on who can be with the mother while she is giving birth. There is also little space in one hospital room. At home, friends and family are welcome to come and go as the mother **(60)**chooses, not as the hospital dictates.

The number of people allowed to be with the mother is just one restriction hospital policies place on birthing mothers. Freedom from these restrictive policies is **(65)**probably the best part of giving birth at home. Hospitals require birthing mothers to eat nothing more than ice chips during labor, so that the mother's stomach is empty in case she needs general **(70)**anesthesia for an emergency Cesarean. This deliberate starvation causes the mother to lose the energy she needs to deliver the baby, which in turn increases **(75)**the need for a Cesarean section. Furthermore, hospitals require women to lie down in bed for electronic monitoring of the baby. This electronic vigilance allows

fewer nurses to be on staff and provides
(80)insurance companies with a record of
the baby's health. However, it prevents the
mother from walking—a natural way of
using motion and gravity to facilitate the
birthing process. Finally, hospitals
(85)routinely use drugs which severely
affect the unborn or newborn child, causing the mother to be less able to enter contractions or use the Lamaze method.
These practices can benefit some women,
(90)but when they are empirically applied
to all women across the board, they can
make labor more strenuous. Under the
care of a midwife at home, a woman has
more flexibility with procedures that aid
(95)her unique birth.

For women who are experiencing
medical problems in the birth process,
hospitals provide the necessary interven-
tions to save lives. However, these
(100)interventions are unnecessary for a
normal, healthy birth. In this case, a
woman can have a wonderful birth experience with loved ones nurturing her in her
own home and with a knowledgeable
(105)midwife attending to her needs.

7. The use in line 10 of the term "age-old wisdom" refers to

A. common knowledge that ordinary
people have used for centuries.
B. the latest gossip.
C. ignorance and superstition.
D. previous beliefs about midwifery.
E. what people used to think about giving
birth.

8. In line 25, "predator" most likely means

A. the doe's mate.
B. human hunters.
C. animals that feed on deer.
D. scientists.
E. the deer's other young.

9. In lines 55–58, the author describes hospitals
as being

A. mean and uncaring.
B. sterile and professional.
C. warm and compassionate.
D. cold and impersonal.
E. family oriented and considerate.

10. The central contrast between the wilderness
in paragraph 2 and the hospital in
paragraph 3 is best described in which
terms?

A. theory versus practice
B. natural versus technological
C. imaginary versus reality
D. expectation versus result
E. nature versus modern medicine

11. By reading lines 61–63, we can infer that the
author assumed which of the following?

A. Family members are welcome in
hospitals.
B. Hospitals have contempt for a pregnant
woman's family.
C. Doctors have no reason to bar family
members from delivery rooms.
D. Family members will want to closely
participate in childbirth.
E. Most doctors have never participated in
childbirth.

12. The passage serves mainly to

A. inform readers about the dangers of
midwifery.
B. argue that hospitals are unclean places
for childbirth.
C. discuss the history of childbirth
practices.
D. argue for natural childbirth performed
at home.
E. contrast birth in the wild with birth in
man's society.

13. "Cesarean sections," as described in lines 70–75, involve

A. midwives.

B. complicated medical procedures.

C. painful labor techniques.

D. doctors working with midwives.

E. extra rooms in the hospital.

14. Which of the following, if true, would undermine the author's argument about the virtues of natural childbirth at home?

A. Births in hospitals are less susceptible to infection or complications.

B. More infants die in hospitals than at home.

C. People go to hospitals to die.

D. Doctors do not like children.

E. Midwives know more about babies than doctors.

15. The author mentions contractions and Lamaze in order to

A. gives examples of natural childbirth techniques.

B. support the worth of a Cesarean section.

C. prove her theories about birth in the wild.

D. discredit doctors.

E. show why midwives are better at medicine.

16. In line 90, "empirically" most nearly means

A. only partly.

B. part of an empire.

C. with no exception.

D. only for doctors.

E. only for patients.

17. We can infer from lines 85–88 that hospitals use drugs

A. to charge their patients more money.

B. to ease the pain and transition of mothers and babies alike.

C. to help midwives prepare for their responsibility.

D. only in Caesarian sections.

E. only for mothers using Lamaze.

18. The final paragraph serves largely to

A. refute the claims of the previous paragraphs.

B. offer new and compelling evidence for midwives.

C. launch a shrill attack on the Lamaze method.

D. reassert the claims of the first paragraph.

E. remind people that hospitals are not safe.

19. The tone of the paragraph, in regards to the use of midwives and at-home births, is largely

A. approving and enthused.

B. polite and distanced.

C. helpless and flailing.

D. vaguely hostile.

E. detached and disinterested.

SAT Reading Preparation
Practice Test 3

Directions: For each question in this section, select the best answer from among the given choices.

Each sentence below has one or two blanks, each blank indicating that something has been omitted. Beneath the sentence are five choices, labeled A through E. Choose the word or combination of words that, when placed in the sentence, *best* fits the sentence's meaning.

Example: Bob worried it was only a matter of time before Katie_____; she'd been enthusiastic about the plan yesterday, but he expected her to feel differently once she gave the idea serious _____.

A. wavered… decision
B. obliged… hesitation
C. demurred… consideration
D. argued… rethinking
E. exited… reconciliation

The correct answer is *C*.

1. We were _____ people who could sit in silence for long stretches and not feel uncomfortable.
   A. taciturn
   B. ubiquitous
   C. antagonistic
   D. effusive
   E. flagrant

2. I respect Stearns county people for their _____; they may look down on strangers but they look down on all of them _____.
   A. antimony… uncritically
   B. antipathy… specially
   C. egocentrism… egregiously
   D. egalitarianism… equally
   E. industry… industriously

3. Larry is a(n) _____ student: he is way behind on his homework assignments.
   A. erudite
   B. energetic
   C. steadfast
   D. recalcitrant
   E. indolent

4. Although birth and marriage are attended by no special ritual, _____ lie at the core of Aboriginal culture.
   A. jobs
   B. traditions
   C. passages
   D. politics
   E. parties

5. While the professor spoke _____ about the novel he was beginning, his students showed no special interest in his _____.
   A. passionately….endeavor
   B. earnestly…position
   C. passively…book
   D. responsibly…musings
   E. truthfully…hobbies

The passages below are followed by questions based on content. Questions following a pair of related passages may also ask how the passages relate to one another. Answer the questions below on the basis of what is *stated* or *implied* in the passages as well as any introductory material provided.

Questions 6–7 are based on this passage:

A chance discovery in a pile of papyrus has uncovered what some believe to be the earliest example of a common hygiene product: toothpaste. Dr. Hermann (5)Harrauer, the head of research for the papyrus collection, reported finding a formula for tooth cleaning. The formula is estimated to have been written almost 1,700 years ago, in the Fourth century (10)AD.

The Grecian formula is considered to be ahead of its time when compared to other teeth-cleaning devices and mixtures used centuries later. Some dentists have (15)even called the ingredients "advanced." The formula, written in Greek, consists of minute amounts of rock salt, mint, a dried iris flower, and 20 grains of pepper. When mixed and placed (20)in the mouth, saliva makes it into what is called a "clean toothpaste." Tests had to be made to substantiate the claims of dentists extolling the virtues of this find. Some dentists have actually tried the (25)paste. Two reported that while the concoction made their gums bleed, it was a "big improvement" on other formulas, even those invented as recently as a century ago. At that time, soap and chalk (30)were the two key ingredients of toothpaste. By way of comparison, toothpaste today is highly chemical, a mix of sodium fluoride, the whitener Triclosan, and any number of flavorings. Meanwhile, a trend **(35)**towards using natural ingredients in toothpaste, including baking soda, has sparked an interest in one ancient ingredient. Modern dentists have rediscovered the iris as a natural tool in fighting gum **(40)**disease, leading to its use in some recent products.

6. The author's primary purpose in the passage is to

   A. question the quality and effectiveness of modern toothpaste.

   B. inform dentists of the cleaning properties of the iris.

   C. question the validity of Dr. Hermann Harrauer's discovery.

   D. inform the reader of the recent discovery of a Grecian toothpaste formula.

   E. suggest natural products are more beneficial than artificial.

7. Lines 10–14 suggest the author would most likely agree with which of the following statements?

   A. Ancient formulas for toothpaste are inferior to modern formulas.

   B. Ancient Greeks paid more attention to oral hygiene than other ancient cultures.

   C. The Grecian formula could be used to improve toothpaste today.

   D. Grecian society was intellectually advanced.

   E. Greek inventions have historically been overrated.

Questions 8–9 are based on this passage:

Excerpt from "The Enchanted Bluff" by Willa Cather

We had our swim before sundown, and while we were cooking our supper the oblique rays of light made a dazzling glare on the white sand about us. The **(5)**translucent red ball itself sank behind the brown stretches of cornfield as we sat down to eat, and the warm layer of air that had rested over the water and our clean sandbar grew fresher and smelled of the **(10)**rank ironweed and sunflowers growing on the flatter shore. The river was brown and sluggish, like any other of·the half-dozen streams that water the Nebraska corn lands. On one shore was an **(15)**irregular line of bald clay bluffs where a few scrub oaks with thick trunks and flat, twisted tops threw light shadows on the long grass. The western shore was low and level, with cornfields that stretched to **(20)**the skyline, and all along the water's edge were little sandy coves and beaches where slim cottonwoods and willow saplings flickered.

8. Which one of the following can be inferred from the passage?

   A. The beach is littered with debris.

   B. The river is contaminated.

   C. The beach is surrounded by corn.

   D. The beach is a violent place.

   E. The beach is a peaceful place.

9. The author uses hyperbole in lines 19–20 in order to

A. emphasize the breadth and height of the cornfields around the river.

B. introduce a discussion of the unusual height of cornfields in Nebraska.

C. juxtapose the height of the corn with the shoreline.

D. suggest the cornfields were swaying in the wind.

E. emphasize the rural setting of the passage.

Questions 10–17 are based on this passage:

Though not as popular among history enthusiasts as its "sequel" in the 1940s, the First World War, also known as World War I and (ironically) The War to End All (5)Wars, had just as much an impact on modern civilization. The war began on June 28, 1914, when an obscure and minor Austrian noble named Archduke Francis Ferdinand (heir to the throne of Austria-(10)Hungary) was visiting Sarajevo, the capital of his empire's province of Bosnia. Gavrilo Princep, a Serbian nationalist who wanted Bosnia to be part of Serbia, shot the Archduke and his wife after they left a (15)parade route and became lost. Austria-Hungary accused its neighbor, Serbia, of plotting to kill the Archduke and threatened war. Russia, which was allied with Serbia, threatened war with Austria-(20)Hungary. Germany supported Austria-Hungary, and France mobilized its forces to help Russia.

By that August, Germany and Austria-Hungary were at war with France and Russia. Crucial to Germany's strategy was the conquering of neutral Belgium and (25)crippling France. When Germany attacked Belgium, Great Britain entered the war on the side of France and Russia, forming the military alliance known as the Triple Entente. Germany attacked France,

(30)coming within visual range of Paris, until the French stopped their advance at the hideously costly Battle of the Marne (1914). For their next tactic, the French dug trenches as defensive positions, a (35)technique theorized sixty years earlier but not put into common practice. The Germans did the same, and soon lines of opposing trenches stretched from Switzerland to the North Sea, long gashes in the (40)earth that teemed with men and equipment as well as germs and disease.

Over the next three years, each side's army hunkered down, digging in and constantly fortifying their trenches. In between lay the notorious "No Man's (45)Land"—a stretch of blighted earth strewn with landmines, barbed wire, and other booby traps. When each side introduced machine guns and poison gas, the war turned especially deadly. Firing (50)bullets in uncannily rapid succession, soldiers used machine guns to shoot massive amounts of ammunition at the enemy in a short amount of time, increasing accuracy a thousand fold. Deadly canisters of (55)mustard gas, first used by the Germans, killed or disabled soldiers instantly. Artillery shells carried the gas to the enemy. As the artillery exploded, gas would engulf the soldiers, liquefying their (60)internal organs and leaving them struggling for breath. Often the gas destroyed the soldiers' lungs, causing them to fill with fluid, literally drowning them from the inside out. Soldiers died by (65)the hundreds of thousands. In the Battle of Verdun, which lasted six months in 1916, 550,000 men died on the French and British side. Some 434,000 men died on the German side.

(70)Another important development in the war was the use of the airplane. In 1909, Wilbur and Orville Wright built the first functioning airplane. By World War I, the warring powers on the Western Front (75)used over 400 aircraft. At the beginning of the war, nations used these planes primarily for scouting and reconnaissance. By the end of the conflict, countries equipped airplanes with machine guns that (80)could fire through an aircraft's propeller and attack enemy aircraft.

From the war's outset, the people of the United States took the position of neutrality. President Woodrow Wilson—who (85)ran for reelection in 1916 on the slogan "He Kept Us Out of War"—urged Americans to resist the constant propaganda coming from both sides. However, many events and factors pushed the (90)United States toward declaring war against Germany. For example, numerous business interests were tied to Great Britain, as it supplied the nation with weapons and other supplies. Corporations were (95)eager for a war effort also because the nation was in a period of high unemployment. With a war, employment and productivity would increase. Moreover, wealthy bankers such as J. P. Morgan had (100)loaned millions of dollars to Great Britain as it fought Germany. The banking elite had a vested interest in seeing Great Britain win the war and repay the loans with interest. Still, the United States (105)watched the war from a distance, only involving itself once a German submarine sank the American-laden passenger ship *Lusitania* in May 1917.

10. The word "outset" in line 82 most nearly means
   A. cause of.
   B. beginning.
   C. end.
   D. viewpoint
   E. attack.

11. The description of the effects of mustard gas in lines 61–66 serve to
   A. demonstrate the hostility the war produced.
   B. incite the reader to hate Germans.
   C. show how warfare in World War I was cruel and painful.
   D. relate one soldier's experiences.
   E. foreshadow the outcome of the war.

12. The first paragraph serves primarily to
   A. complain enough people don't know enough about WWI.
   B. assert that more wars like WWI are inevitable.
   C. assert that WWI remains important and explain its start.
   D. explain that the events in the essay happened a long time ago.
   E. illustrate the destruction WWI wreaked on Europe.

13. The author's assertion about the wealthy bankers in lines 102–104 would be most weakened if which of the following were true?
   A. Britain didn't want to repay its loans.
   B. The debts were paid by private citizens.
   C. America also owed money to Britain.
   D. Germany and Austria-Hungary also owed America money.
   E. The interest payments would be waved if Germany won the war.

14. The author uses the phrase "a stretch of blighted earth strewn with landmines, barbed wire, and other booby traps" in lines 45– 47 to depict
   A. how deadly the two armies' weapons had become.
   B. that no one wanted to fight for the land.
   C. why America wouldn't enter the war.
   D. the land was uninhabitable.
   E. German ingenuity in building weapons.

15. According to the fifth paragraph, we can infer that the people of the United States, prior to the sinking of the *Lusitania,* were

A. uninterested in the war.

B. passionate to go to war.

C. ready to believe anything the president told them.

D. interested in but slow to take sides in a European war.

E. hoping the French would win.

16. The author's tone in the paragraph can best be described as

A. morose.   D. hostile.

B. captivated.   E. scholarly.

C. uninformed.

17. The author would most likely agree with all of the following EXCEPT

A. WWI was a great waste of human life.

B. events this many years ago have no impact on us today.

C. the United States was right to intervene in WWI.

D. WWI saw great advancements in technology and weapons.

E. such worldwide conflicts should not happen again.

Questions 18–24 are based on this passage:

The *feminist* or *women's liberation movement* is a social and political movement that sought equality of rights and societal status for women. Key goals of (5)this movement include giving women the freedom to choose their own careers and increased freedom to determine their own lifestyles. The history of the women's rights movement goes back to the 1840s, (10)when activists such as Elizabeth Stanton, Susan Anthony, and Lucretia Mott advocated greater rights for women. Few were willing to accept as radical a change as that suggested by Stanton and Anthony, (15)particularly Stanton's notion that laws that facilitated an inferior position for women were inherently unjust. Views, like that of Catherine Beecher, accepting that a woman's sphere was in the domestic (20)realm but that women should still receive an education, had more general appeal. As the decades progressed, the women's rights movement made some advances at the state and local levels, but (25)conditions remained fundamentally unchanged. Beginning in the 1980s, women began entering the workforce in unprecedented numbers—not so much because of the women's rights movement (30)but because of economic pressure for a family to have a second income. This event led to gradual advances, such as women's ability to work outside the three common female positions of teacher, (35)nurse, and domestic servant. Still, except for a few rare exceptions, women remained in those jobs or in clerical and sales positions.

Shortly after World War I, the (40)movement was able to achieve the aim at the forefront of its concerns—suffrage, or "the vote"—with the passing of the 19$^\text{th}$ Amendment to the U.S. Constitution. Gaining access to the ballot-box (45)would put women in a position to make other changes over time, but the most radical of the advances would be ushered in side-by-side with the civil rights movement.

(50)In the 1960s, the push for women's rights largely grew up from the grass-roots level, but new government laws and policies also had a profound impact. At the suggestion of Esther (55)Peterson, director of the Women's Bureau of the Department of Labor, President John F. Kennedy set up the first national Commission on the Status of

Women in 1962. The following year, the **(60)**commission reported epidemic employment discrimination, unequal pay, legal inequality, and insufficient enforcement mechanisms for working women with grievances. The commission's report **(65)**led to the Equal Pay Act of 1963, which made it illegal to pay lesser wages to a woman doing the same work as a man. The new law had limited effect, however, because most women remained **(70)**in traditionally female occupations that offered low wages and few opportunities for advancement. In 1963, women were paid, on average, 41 percent less than men. Title VII of the Civil Rights Act **(75)**of 1964 prohibited employment discrimination based on gender as well as race, color, or ethnic origin. The act also established the equal Employment Opportunity Commission (EEOC) to enforce the **(80)**new law.

Noted feminist Betty Friedan presented the results of her research on American women in a book entitled *The Feminine Mystique* (1963). Friedan's book **(85)**presented the interesting finding that housewives were not the happy and completely satisfied homemakers as they were portrayed in magazines and television. In 1966, she helped found the National **(90)**Organization of Women (NOW) and served as its first president. NOW promotes the equality of men and women through legislation, rallies, marches, and support for like-minded political **(95)**candidates. Gloria Steinem, a journalist and publisher, became a leader in the feminist movement in the late 1960s. With Betty Friedan and Shirley Chisholm (the first black woman elected to Congress), **(100)**Steinem helped found the National Women's Political Caucus (1971) to encourage women to seek political office and to work for women's rights laws. Friedan, Steinem, and NOW supported a **(105)**new amendment to the Constitution, the Equal Rights Amendment (ERA), which would have guaranteed women equal rights. Congress passed the ERA in 1972 and extended the deadline for states' **(110)**ratification by three years, but the ERA ultimately failed to become an official part of the Constitution.

18. This passage is concerned primarily with
    A. the Civil Rights Movement.
    B. the struggle for equal pay for women.
    C. efforts by the government to curb women's rights.
    D. the life of Betty Friedan.
    E. the history of the women's liberation movement.

19. From the passage, we can infer that the women's right movement has
    A. grown in fits and starts in the country's history.
    B. never really gained popular support.
    C. become an antiquated way of thinking.
    D. reached all its goals and disbanded.
    E. concentrated on electing a woman president.

20. All of the following were goals of the women's rights movements EXCEPT
    A. the right to vote.
    B. the freedom to select their own careers.
    C. the freedom to determine their own lifestyles.
    D. the right to run for public office.
    E. the right to equal pay.

21. In context, "grass-roots" most nearly means
    A. vested interest groups.
    B. big business.
    C. ordinary citizens.
    D. wealthy policy makers.
    E. government officials.

22. Based on the passage, what was the 19ᵗʰ Amendment and when was it passed, respectively?
    A. insured equal pay for equal work, 1962
    B. the right to own property, 1880
    C. banned employment discrimination, 1963
    D. the right to vote, 1920
    E. protection from unfair labor practices, 1972

23. Based on the passage, we can infer that the prominent figures of the women's movement in the 1840s
    A. were united in their cause.
    B. were concerned with maintaining the status quo.
    C. had differing ideas of the roles of women in society.
    D. held beliefs that were representative of all women at the time.
    E. all believed women were governed by laws that were unjust.

24. In 1962, the Commission on the Status of Women found evidence of all of the following work-related issues for women EXCEPT
    A. employment discrimination.
    B. legal inequality.
    C. insufficient enforcement mechanism for working women with grievances.
    D. unequal pay.
    E. inhumane working conditions.

Section II

24 Questions

Time – 25 Minutes

For each question in this section, select the best answer from the choices given and fill in the corresponding blank.

Each sentence below has one or two blanks, each blank indicating that something has been omitted. Beneath the sentence are five choices, labeled A through E. Choose the word or combination of words that, when placed in the sentence, *best* fits the sentence's meaning.

1. Winning the World Series was a monumental achievement for the Red Sox, _____ in a grand parade through the downtown streets of Boston.
    A. extending   D. culminating
    B. resulting   E. collapsing
    C. expanding

2. Looking to _____ the dispute with his irate landlord, the _____ tenant proposed an agreeable solution to their disagreement.
    A. settle…enamored
    B. reconcile…conscientious
    C. resolve…disinterested
    D. compound…unruly
    E. ameliorate…lackluster

3. At the _____ of the Civil War, the North was a very strong industrial region, whereas the South consisted largely of farms and small towns.
   A. center
   B. outbreak
   C. revival
   D. result
   E. midpoint

4. Although their parents and relatives considered the Johnson children lovable and _____, their classmates knew them to be _____ and mean-spirited.
   A. considerate…manipulative
   B. compassionate…mature
   C. bright…lonely
   D. adventurous…disinterested
   E. kind…ignorant

5. Using aerial survey photography and a network of scientist informants, anthropologists _____ that little more than a million elephants now exist in Africa.
   A. guess
   B. hope
   C. deny
   D. theorize
   E. intimate

6. Joseph needed approval from his professor that his thesis had merit, so he _____ the help of his counselor and graduate school dean to plead his case.
   A. enlisted
   B. refuted
   C. summoned
   D. reasoned
   E. developed

7. Despite _____ requests for aid and assistance, the hurricane victims were often left to _____ for themselves when it came to their ultimate survival.
   A. rude…forage
   B. many…endure
   C. repeated…fend
   D. habitual…scrounge
   E. unanswered…shop

8. Victory at the Battle of Midway was the turning point for America in the war against Japan, crippling the Japanese navy and _____ the United States to gain a decisive _____ in the Pacific Theater during World War II.
   A. enabling…advantage
   B. causing…defeat
   C. bringing…gain
   D. allowing…retreat
   E. pushing…weakness

The passages below are followed by questions based on content. Questions following a pair of related passages may also ask how the passages relate to one another. Answer the questions below on the basis of what is *stated* or *implied* in the passages as well as any introductory material provided.

Questions 9–12 are based on the following passages:

Passage 1

Taken from Andrew Carnegie's "The Gospel of Wealth"

The problem of our age is the administration of wealth, so that the ties of brotherhood may still bind together the rich and poor in harmonious relationship. **(5)**The conditions of human life have not only been changed, but revolutionized, within the past few hundred years. In former days there was little difference between the dwelling, dress, **(5)**food, and **(10)**environment of the chief and those of his retainers [. . .] The contrast between the palace of the millionaire and the cottage of the laborer with us today measures the change which has come with **(15)**civilization.

This change, however, is not to be deplored, but welcomed as highly beneficial. It is well, nay, essential for the progress of the race, that the houses of **(20)**some should be homes for all that is highest and best in literature and the arts, and for all the refinements of civilization, rather than that none should be so. Much better this great irregularity than universal **(25)**squalor [. . .] The "good old times" were not good old times. Neither master nor servant was as well situated then as today. A relapse to old conditions would be disastrous to both—not the least so to **(30)**him who serves—and would sweep away civilization with it...

Passage 2

Taken from Henry David Thoreau's "Walden"

Most men, even in this comparatively free country, through mere ignorance and mistake, are so occupied with the factitious cares and superfluously coarse **(35)**labors of life that its finer fruits cannot be plucked by them. Their fingers, from excessive toil, are too clumsy and tremble too much for that. Actually, the laboring man has not leisure for a true integrity day **(40)**by day; he cannot afford to sustain the manliest relations to men; his labor would be depreciated in the market. He has no time to be anything but a machine. How can he remember well his ignorance— **(45)**which his growth requires—who has so often to use his knowledge? We should feed and clothe him gratuitously sometimes, and recruit him with our cordials, before we judge of him. The finest **(50)**qualities of our nature, like the bloom on fruits, can be preserved only by the most delicate handling. Yet we do not treat ourselves nor one another thus tenderly.

Some of you, we all know, are poor, **(55)**find it hard to live, are sometimes, as it were, gasping for breath. I have no doubt that some of you who read this book are unable to pay for all the dinners which you have actually eaten, or for the coats **(60)**and shoes which are fast wearing or are already worn out, and have come to this page to spend borrowed or stolen time, robbing your creditors of an hour. It

is very evident what mean and sneaking
(65)lives many of you live, for my sight
has been whetted by experience; always
on the limits, trying to get into business
and trying to get out of debt, a very
ancient slough . . . called by the Latins *æs*
(70)*alienum*, "another's brass", for some
of their coins were made of brass; still living, and dying, and buried by this other's
brass; always promising to pay, promising
to pay, tomorrow, and dying today…

9. Which of the following best describes the
   relationship between the two passages?

   A. Passage 2 refutes the argument in
      Passage 1.

   B. Passage 1 directly attacks the argument
      in Passage 2.

   C. Passage 2 supports the argument in
      Passage 1.

   D. Passage 1 is broad and universal; Pas-
      sage 2 is detailed and complex.

   E. Passage 1 provides an explanation for
      the problem posed in Passage 2.

10. The words "chief," "retainers," "master,"
    and "servant" are used primarily in Passage
    1 in order to

    A. underscore the extent of the differences
       between the rich and the poor today.

    B. suggest the disparity between the rich
       and the poor is continuing.

    C. explain the need for a wealthy few and
       countless poor.

    D. suggest the harmony between the
       wealthy and the poor is increasing.

    E. emphasize the changing relationship
       between the wealthy and the poor
       through the centuries.

11. The simile "like the bloom on fruits" in
    Passage 2 is mainly intended to

    A. be taken literally.

    B. criticize humanity's cruelty.

    C. suggest the frail nature of humanity.

    D. emphasize humanity's mortality.

    E. suggest the comparison is
       metaphorical.

12. In Passage 2, "superfluously" most nearly
    means

    A. superficially.

    B. abundantly.

    C. hazardously.

    D. apprehensively.

    E. radically.

**Questions 13–24 are based on the following
passage:**

*The following is excerpted from "The Red-Headed
League," a short story by Sir Arthur Conan Doyle.
Dr. Watson, friend of Sherlock Holmes, is the
narrator of this story. Watson has arrived at
Holmes' apartment while Holmes is meeting with a
client.*

The portly client puffed out his chest
with an appearance of some little pride
and pulled a dirty and wrinkled newspaper
from the inside pocket of his greatcoat. As
(5)he glanced down the advertisement column, with his head thrust forward and the
paper flattened out upon his knee, I took a
good look at the man and endeavored,
after the fashion of my companion, to read
(10)the indications which might be presented by his dress or appearance.

I did not gain very much, however, by
my inspection. Our visitor bore every
mark of being an average commonplace
(15) British tradesman, obese, pompous,
and slow. He wore rather baggy gray shepherd's check trousers, a not over-clean

black frock-coat, unbuttoned in the front, and a drab waistcoat with a heavy brassy (20)Albert chain, and a square pierced bit of metal dangling down as an ornament. A frayed top-hat and a faded brown overcoat with a wrinkled velvet collar lay upon a chair beside him. Altogether, look as I (25)would, there was nothing remarkable about the man save his blazing red head, and the expression of extreme chagrin and discontent upon his features.

Sherlock Holmes's quick eye took in (30)my occupation, and he shook his head with a smile as he noticed my questioning glances. "Beyond the obvious facts that he has at some time done manual labour, that he takes snuff, that he is a Freemason, that (35)he has been in China, and that he has done a considerable amount of writing lately, I can deduce nothing else."

Mr. Jabez Wilson started up in his chair, with his forefinger upon the paper, (40)but his eyes upon my companion.

"How, in the name of good-fortune, did you know all that, Mr. Holmes?" he asked. "How did you know, for example, that I did manual labour. It's as true as (45)gospel, for I began as a ship's carpenter."

"Your hands, my dear sir. Your right hand is quite a size larger than your left. You have worked with it, and the muscles (50)are more developed."

"Well, the snuff, then, and the Free-masonry?"

"I won't insult your intelligence by telling you how I read that, especially as, (55)rather against the strict rules of your order, you use an arc-and-compass breast-pin."

Oh, of course, I forgot that. But the writing?"

(60)"What else can be indicated by that right cuff so very shiny for five inches, and the left one with the smooth patch near the elbow where you rest it upon the desk?"

(65)"Well, but China?"

"The fish that you have tattooed immediately above your right wrist could only have been done in China. I have made a small study of tattoo marks and (70)have even contributed to the literature of the subject. That trick of staining the fishes' scales of a delicate pink is quite peculiar to China. When, in addition, I see a Chinese coin hanging from your watch-(75)chain, the matter becomes even more simple."

Mr. Jabez Wilson laughed heavily. "Well, I never!" said he. "I thought at first (80)that you had done something clever, but I see that there was nothing in it, after all."

"I begin to think, Watson," said Holmes, "that I make a mistake in (85)explaining. '*Omne ignotum pro magnifico**,' you know, and my poor little reputation, such as it is, will suffer shipwreck if I am so candid."

*"Everything unknown is assumed to be magnificent."

13. What is the primary purpose of the passage?

   A. to demonstrate Holmes's uncanny ability of observation

   B. to question Watson's loyalty to Holmes

   C. to validate Wilson's occupation as a Freemason

   D. to contradict Holmes's original assumption of his client

   E. to illustrate Holmes's mistakes as a detective

14. As used in line 27, the word "chagrin" most nearly means

A. criticism. D. cognizance.

B. embarrassment. E. cruelty.

C. stimulation.

15. How did Holmes conclude Wilson was a manual laborer?

A. Wilson had a tattoo of a hammer on his arm.

B. Holmes had seen Wilson working on a ship the day before.

C. Wilson's right hand was larger than his left.

D. Wilson wore a pin on his lapel with the symbol for labor.

E. Watson told Holmes that Mr. Wilson had once been a ship's carpenter.

16. In lines 70–71, Holmes mentions he's "contributed to the literature of the subject" of tattoos in order to

A. prove that he's an authority on tattoos.

B. convince Wilson the man is a criminal.

C. prove he's the world's greatest detective.

D. shock the man into a confession.

E. make Wilson go away.

17. In the context of the passage, Wilson's statement "I see there was nothing in it…" (line 81) suggests his

A. amazement at Holmes' skill.

B. annoyance at Wilson's eavesdropping.

C. desire to be cleared of a crime.

D. relief that Holmes wasn't practicing magic.

E. anger that Holmes had found him out.

18. In lines 17–18, "a not over-clean frock coat" emphasizes how Watson looks on Wilson as

A. fussy about his appearance.

B. typical of the unkempt British working classes.

C. probably a criminal.

D. some new friend of Holmes'.

E. a British seaman at home from abroad.

19. The passage is best described as

A. a list of clues, with accompanying explanation.

B. a long treatise on the British middle-class.

C. an exposé on Watson's snobbery.

D. a complete mystery.

E. the end of a plot.

20. As used in line 37, "deduce" most nearly means

A. assume. D. ignore.

B. embody. E. ruminate.

C. flatter.

21. In line 30, Holmes "shook his head…" in order to

A. answer Watson's unspoken questions.

B. dismiss Watson's judgment.

C. make Watson go away.

D. reassure Wilson.

E. indicate he'd solved the story's mystery.

22. Which of the following, if true, would most undermine the validity of Holmes' conclusions about Wilson's tattoos?

A. Not all tattoos come from China.

B. The tattoo artist was studying Chinese techniques.

C. A shop in London was doing fish tattoos.

D. A tattoo shop in London was copying Chinese techniques.

E. The tattoo was a temporary fake.

23. All of the following is true of Wilson EXCEPT that

   A.   he has spent time in China.

   B.   his pin indicates he is a Freemason.

   C.   he once captained a sailing vessel.

   D.   his clothes are disheveled.

   E.   he spends much of his time writing.

24. In the context of the passage, we might infer that Holmes expresses his feelings in Latin because

   A.   he doesn't want Wilson to understand his secret.

   B.   he wants to sound smart.

   C.   Watson only speaks Latin fluently.

   D.   Latin is the language of detectives.

   E.   he wants the meaning to appear important and secret.

Section III

19 Questions

Time – 20 Minutes

For each question in this section, select the best answer from the choices given and fill in the corresponding blank.

Each sentence below has one or two blanks, each blank indicating that something has been omitted. Beneath the sentence are five choices, labeled A through E. Choose the word or

1. The Donner Party was on the brink of starving to death in the mountains of Utah; their only _____ was to _____ what little food they had among the survivors.

   A.   question…see

   B.   answer…divide

   C.   problem…decide

   D.   recourse…ration

   E.   idea…consume

2. Politicians make speeches promising educational _____, but conditions in our public schools continue to worsen each year.

   A.   taxation

   B.   destruction

   C.   importance

   D.   forgiveness

   E.   reform

3. The _____ autumn made everyone curious; perhaps there was some truth in scientists _____ about global warming.

   A.   freezing…. bragging

   B.   typical… crying

   C.   temperate… warning

   D.   broiling… cheering

   E.   silent… laughing

4. Though _____ and coy when she went on dates, Lisa confused the young men pursuing her by acting _____ when they called her again.

   A.   sullen… interested

   B.   flirtatious… disinterested

   C.   friendly… desperate

   D.   sleepy… hopeful

   E.   inviting… grateful

5. The hallmark of a truly _____ man is the ability to remain focused and civilized, even against _____ odds.
   A. unhealthy… daunting
   B. intelligent… favorable
   C. deliberate… imposing
   D. valiant… daunting
   E. brave… dwindling

6. When in autumn of 1937 Hitler was _____ the incorporation of Austria and Czechoslovakia into the Third Reich, he knew all along that he was _____ a major war.
   A. considering…instigating
   B. pondering…escaping
   C. resolving…discussing
   D. avoiding…deciding
   E. restructuring…avoiding

The passages below are followed by questions based on content. Answer the questions below on the basis of what is *stated* or *implied* in the passages as well as any introductory material provided.

Questions 7–19 are based on the following passages:

Passage 1

Excerpt from "The beauty of literature," in *The Psychology of Beauty*, by Ethel D. Puffer

Now the word is nothing in itself; it is not sound primarily, but thought. The word is but a sign, a negligible quantity in human intercourse—a counter in which the coins are ideas (5)and emotions—merely legal tender, of no value save in exchange. What we really experience in the sound of a sentence, in the sight of a printed page, is a complex sequence of visual and other images, ideas, emotions, (10)feelings, logical relations, swept along in the stream of consciousness,—differing, indeed, in certain ways from daily experience, but yet primarily of the web of life itself. The words in their nuances, march, tempo, melody add certain (15)elements to this flood—hasten, retard, undulate, or calm it; but it is the THOUGHT, the understood experience, that is the stuff of literature.

Words are first of all meanings, and meanings (20)are to be understood and lived through. We can hardly even speak of the meaning of a word, but rather of what it is, directly, in the mental state that is called up by it. Every definition of a word is but a feeble and distant (25)approximation of the unique flash of experience belonging to that word. It is not the sound sensation nor the visual image evoked by the word which counts, but the whole of the mental experience, to which the word is but an (30)occasion and a cue. Therefore, since literature is the art of words, it is the stream of thought itself that we must consider as the material of literature. In short, literature is the dialect of life—as Stevenson said; it is by (35)literature that the business of life is carried on. Some one, however, may here demur: visual signs, too, are the dialect of life. We understand by what we see, and we live by what we understand. The curve of a line, the crescendo of (40)a note, serve also for wordless messages. Why are not, then, painting and music the vehicles of experience, and to be judged first as evocation of life, and only afterward as sight and hearing? This conceded, we are thrown back on

(45)that view of art as "the fixed quantity of imaginative thought supplemented by certain technical qualities,—of color in painting, of sound in music, of rhythmical words in poetry," from which it has been the one aim of the (50)preceding arguments of this book to free us.

Passage 2

Excerpt from "Literature and Life," in *Escape and Other Essays*, by Arthur Christopher Benson

There is a tendency, not by any means among the greater writers, but among what may be called the epigoni,—the satellites of literature, the men who would be great if they knew how,—to speak (5)of the business of writing as if it were a sacred mystery, pontifically celebrated, something remote and secret, which must be guarded from the vulgar and the profane, and which requires an initiation to comprehend. I always feel rather (10)suspicious of this attitude; it seems to me something of a pose, adopted in order to make other people envious and respectful. It is the same sort of precaution as the "properties" of the wizard, his gown and wand, the stuffed crocodile (15)and the skeleton in the corner; for if there is a great fuss made about locking and double-locking a box, it creates a presumption of doubt as to whether there is anything particular in it. In my nursery days one of my brothers was fond of (20)locking up his private treasures in a box, producing it in public, unfastening it, glancing into it with a smile, and then softly closing it and turning the key in a way calculated to provoke the most intense curiosity as to the contents; but (25)upon investigation it proved to contain nothing but the wool of sheep, dried beans, and cases of exploded cartridges.

So, too, I have known both writers and artists who made a mystery out of their craft, professed (30)a holy rapture, as if the business of imagination and the art of setting things down were processes that could not be explained to ordinary people, but were the property of a brotherhood. And thus grow up cliques and (35)coteries, of people who, by mutual admiration, try to console one another for the absence of the applause which the world will not concede them, and to atone for the coldness of the public by a warmth of intimate proximity.

(40)This does not in the least apply to groups of people who are genuinely and keenly interested in art of any kind, and form a congenial circle in which they discuss, frankly and enthusiastically, methods of work, the books, ideas, pictures, and (45)music which interest them. That is quite a different thing, a real fortress of enthusiasm in the midst of Meshech and Kedar. What makes it base and morbid is the desire to exclude for the sake of exclusion; to indulge in solitary raptures, (50)hoping to be overheard; to keep the tail of the eye upon the public; to attempt to mystify; and to trade upon the inquisitive instinct of human beings, the natural desire, that is, to know what is going on within any group that seems to (55)have exciting business of its own.

7. The word "negligible" (line 3) in Passage 1 is closest in meaning to which of the following words?
   A. small
   B. priceless
   C. considerable
   D. careless
   E. significant

8. According to the author of Passage 1, what is the main component of literature?
   A. intelligence
   B. ideas
   C. sound
   D. vocabulary
   E. imagery

9. In the first paragraph of Passage 1, what literary device is used?

A. hyperbole D. allusion
B. metaphor E. paradox
C. simile

10. The primary purpose of the first paragraph of Passage 1 is to

A. emphasize the importance of word choice in writing.
B. explain how meaningless words can be.
C. make a distinction between words and experience.
D. explain the significance of a word's sound.
E. describe how a word's appearance affects its meaning.

11. The author of Passage 1 would most likely agree with which of the following statements?

A. Any writer can recreate an experience perfectly by using the right words.
B. Each word has one meaning that corresponds to it.
C. The meaning that is found in literature arises out of the meaning of the words themselves.
D. The meaning of a word itself is not the same as the associations belonging to the word.
E. All people make the same mental association when they hear a particular word.

12. In Passage 2, the word "pontifically" (line 6) is closest in meaning to which of the following words?

A. pompously D. timidly
B. excitedly E. secretly
C. modestly

13. In Passage 2, the story about the author's "nursery days" (lines 18-27) compares the young brother to

A. legendary writers.
B. another schoolmate.
C. arrogant yet average writers.
D. the author himself.
E. the general population.

14. The tone of the first paragraph of Passage 2 can be best described as

A. solemn. D. ironic.
B. earnest. E. playful.
C. grave.

15. Which literary device is used in the following quote from Passage 2?

It is the same sort of precaution as the "properties" of the wizard, his gown and wand, the stuffed crocodile and the skeleton in the corner; for if there is a great fuss made about locking and double-locking a box, it creates a presumption of doubt as to whether there is anything particular in it.

A. personification D. hyperbole
B. oxymoron E. alliteration
C. analogy

16. The last paragraph of Passage 2 primarily serves to _____ the author's earlier statements.

A. qualify D. disprove
B. contradict E. ignore
C. refute

17. Which of the following statements explains how Passage 1 and Passage 2 are different?

A. Passage 2 is serious, while Passage 1 is more lighthearted.

B. Passage 2 focuses on writers, while Passage 1 is centered on writing itself.

C. Passage 2 contradicts the ideas expressed in Passage 1.

D. Passage 2 is specific and factual, while Passage 1 is theoretical.

E. Passage 2 proposes a solution to a problem, while Passage 1 presents the author's perspective on a topic.

18. Compared to the author of Passage 2, the author of Passage 1 regards literature with more

A. suspicion.   D. joy.

B. wit.   E. reverence.

C. sarcasm.

19. The authors of Passage 1 and Passage 2 would most likely agree that

A. talented writers are too full of themselves.

B. people do not read good literature often enough.

C. good writers are born, not made.

D. evaluating literature is often a complex task.

E. it is impossible to relate one's experience through writing.